15
MINUTES TO
HAPPINESS

Published by Blink Publishing
3.08, The Plaza,
535 Kings Road,
Chelsea Harbour,
London, SW10 0SZ

www.blinkpublishing.co.uk

facebook.com/blinkpublishing
twitter.com/blinkpublishing

Paperback – 978-1-911600-58-9
eBook – 978-1-911600-61-9

A CIP catalogue of this book is available from the British Library.

Typeset by EnvyDesign Ltd
Printed and bound by Clays Ltd, St Ives Plc

3 5 7 9 10 8 6 4 2

Blink Publishing is an imprint of the Bonnier Publishing Group
www.bonnierpublishing.co.uk

RICHARD NICHOLLS

Creator of the UK's No.1 self-help podcast

15
MINUTES TO
HAPPINESS

Easy, Everyday Exercises to Help You
Be the Best You Can Be

BLINK
bringing you closer

To my wife Dawn, for over twenty years of
love, support and patience.
Thank you.

Contents

INTRODUCTION

Hello to you!

Welcome to my little book. I hope that it can inspire you to take action that helps you to become a happier you. You don't have to be unhappy to gain benefit from the words; they may simply help you to understand a little more about what makes you tick so as to prevent any future problems, or to help you understand others better.

Throughout the book there will be many ideas or exercises written inside some dark boxes, just like this is, for you to practise. These exercises will be varied both in their type and how much time and effort you'll need to put in, but everything should fit nicely into 15 minutes or less (in some cases much less).

I've been working as a therapist in private practice since 2001 and have been absorbing decades of

INTRODUCTION

research to gain a good understanding of what does and what doesn't work when it comes to boosting happiness, so all of these are tried and tested methods of improving your wellbeing.

Since 2011, I've been using my podcast, Motivate Yourself, as a platform to share these ideas to see how they work in the real world, and in listening to the feedback from my thousands of listeners it gives me even more confidence in these concepts.

So even if they might feel out of character or even a little random to you, do recognise that by embracing these ideas you will obtain tools that can boost self-esteem, help you to appreciate life more and regulate your emotions. Once you've mastered these, feel free to tailor them to your own needs and figure out what works best for you.

INTRODUCTION

You can dip in and out of the book and come back to various exercises at random, but, there's also a bit of detail in here about why these things work, which I would advise reading as well. It's very important to understand how these exercises and attitudes will help you, for many reasons but partly to encourage you to take them on.

This is hopefully going to be an interesting and worthwhile journey. On the way we'll meet Chinese pianists, sabre-toothed tigers, The Joneses next door and a plethora of participants in scientific research. Thank you very much for letting me join you for your ride. I'm very happy to be part of your journey that helps you be the best you can be.

So, shall we get started then?

Chapter One

Think Happy, Be Happy

About the Brain

Right at this minute in between your ears, 100 billion neurons are ready to fire off electrical signals. These signals trigger the laboratory in your brain to start creating the most amazing chemical cocktails. It can make dopamine to boost pleasure, it can send signals to the adrenal gland to make you feel as if you need to fight or run away, and it can even trap you in an endless loop of the opera section of 'Bohemian Rhapsody'. Whatever your brain is doing, though, an enormous amount of it is totally unconscious to you. Your brain is continually busy, ticking away in the background outside of your conscious awareness, regulating body temperature at the same time as keeping an ear out for a sabre-toothed tiger. These are our instincts and we wouldn't be here without them; they've kept us alive in one shape or form since we first came down from the trees around six million years ago.

Back then, unconscious instincts were all we had, until evolution developed our brain, giving us problem-solving skills and eventually the ability to worry about whether there's enough charge in our phone battery.

So here we are some six million years later with a three pound lump in our head that instinctively sends signals to the lungs to breathe in and out and make the heart beat 100 thousand times per day. Abilities we were born already knowing how to do. At the same time though, we can also learn a multitude of skills. We can learn how to walk, how to talk and how to hold a pencil – abilities that we weren't born with. But these abilities are just stepping stones to bigger and better things. We can turn walking into amazingly complex gymnastic moves, turn talking into singing the most sophisticated of arias and turn holding a pencil into drawing such intricate artwork that it looks photographic. Yet, complicated as these things are, when they become skills they go beyond conscious thinking, we do them automatically. They become unconscious abilities, just like instincts, which we do without needing to think about them. Being able to perform these abilities unconsciously would have been a very useful evolutionary trick; any species that needed to stand still while it considers its next move is soon to be tiger food, but the one that can run, dodge and throw spears all at the same time is going to do well. So turning conscious abilities into unconscious abilities frees up our brain to do other things. If you've ever driven a familiar route and pulled up at the end of it with very little recollection of the journey, then you've learned a new instinct.

So, given enough repetition, we can do almost anything without thinking, and that's not always a good thing.

Some of the things we repeat until they become automatic will hinder us in life, though. That's when we may think of them as bad habits, which aren't always about speaking with your mouth full or picking your nose.

When I was a teenager I had a skateboard and would skate around and perform little tricks with an average level of skill. I was nothing particularly special but I had good balance. When my son was around ten years old I bought him a skateboard with the expectation that I would demonstrate exactly how to ride it and make him super proud of his cool dad that could ride a skateboard. I'm not sure exactly what happened next or quite why the bottom half of my body wanted to go one way and my top half the other. What I do know is that it hurt when I hit the concrete. I had forgotten how to ride a skateboard – the skill had gone. This reminded me of a friend of mine who, after 20 years, decided to start playing the guitar again. At school he was a very impressive classical guitarist but became bored with it as a teenager – the guitar just couldn't compete with the PlayStation and girls. After all that time away from it, the effort required to get even halfway towards his old skill level again was demotivating and he almost gave up. But he stuck with it; now he plays at open mic nights throughout his town and he's never been happier. But it took a lot of repetition to make it all stick again, because his skills were only conscious skills; the ability to play guitar without thinking had gone. The expression 'If you don't use it, you lose it.' isn't just a catchy rhyme – it's true. It's what happened to me when I stopped skateboarding, it's exactly what happened to my friend when he stopped playing the guitar, and it's precisely what can happen to you if you're ready to unlearn something.

I often use the analogy of a cornfield to represent how to learn and unlearn. Imagine you want to get from point A to point Z in a cornfield, maybe from one corner of the field to another. There is a pathway through the corn, but it's not a straight line. It twists and turns through many other points in the field. The only way to get from A to Z is to go through B, C and D etc. before finally arriving at the right place. This is how the brain connects together over time. It builds all of these points in our brain and fires electrical signals from one to another to create the desired outcome. Let's say you want to put one foot in front of the other and take a step forward. Each time you do that, you need to lift one foot off the floor while shifting your body weight onto the other foot. Your hips will tilt slightly sideways as you bend your knee and you land on your heel, moving your body forward. Then, while your back leg prepares to bend, you straighten the forward leg and repeat the whole process. It uses dozens of muscles, which all receive signals from the brain to contract and relax at the exact right time to make sure that you don't land on your backside. After a lot of repetition, the pathways in the brain, just like a cornfield, become so well trodden that it becomes superfast to get from A to Z. Now, the point of this cornfield analogy is to help you recognise that there may well be other ways of getting from A to Z. You could of course just stand at point A looking directly at point Z and walk in a straight line. But there's corn in the way, so this route will actually take longer than, say, a well-trodden path that doesn't involve trampling on corn. However, if you walk in that straight line from A to Z enough times, it gets easier and easier because the corn gets squashed down a little bit more each time until you've made a whole new pathway to where you want to go. The old pathway then becomes overgrown, you'll hardly be able to use it any more, and you may even forget that it used to be there. I'm over-simplifying neuroscience here, I know. But this is how we learn, and also how we unlearn. Because anything that is repeated enough times becomes habitual, even emotions. Both the good and the bad ones.

Basically, you can get good at feeling bad, so good at it in fact that you may not even be aware that you're doing it to yourself. But the good news is that if you stop practising a bad habit, you can easily forget how to do it. Something that I say a lot to my clients is that a habit that isn't fed is soon dead.

So what would you like to unlearn? What have you learned in the first place that may be preventing you from experiencing the world through happier or more positive eyes? Maybe you've learned to be angry or anxious. Maybe you've learned to be helpless or resentful. Maybe you're not sure what you've learned but you know that you'd like to learn something new. Well, congratulations! Because the fact that you have taken the time to invest in yourself with this book means that you're already a step ahead of everybody else.

So, how do we learn to be happy? Well, firstly it's worth looking at what happiness actually is and then more importantly what it isn't. Happiness is quite subjective: one person may define it as pride and another may think of it as contentment. But the common definition is that happiness is simply a combination of how good you feel on average throughout your day and how satisfied you are with your life as a whole. Crucially for social psychologists studying wellbeing, these are criteria that can be measured, and so over time, studies have been undertaken to find out what works and what doesn't when it comes to altering how good we feel and how satisfied we are. It's long been assumed that, because of the chemistry laboratory in our brain, the ability to be naturally happy or unhappy is something that we're born with, and there is some truth in that. Yes, there is a genetic component to our happiness levels in the same way that there is also a genetic component to our fitness levels. So, in the same way that someone who doesn't have strong athletic genes has to work quite hard to keep fit, someone without strong happiness genes also has to work quite hard at keeping happy.

Research with identical and non-identical twins has shown that around 50% of our mood is controlled by our genetics.[1] So if you've inherited Uncle George's misery guts gene, then almost half of your mood is predetermined and unshakable. It gives you what is called your 'set point' of happiness.

This means that no matter how good or bad life can be, you always return back to this set point eventually.

The other 50% is down to two specific things. The first is your life experiences. Having your legs amputated after a car accident or winning a fortune on the lottery will, of course, alter your mood.

The second is your behaviour and thought processes, such as listening to your favourite music and being optimistic.

Out of those two, which of them has the most influence over our general happiness? Is it the ups and downs of everyday life? Or is it our behaviour and thoughts?

By a huge difference, the greatest influence on our level of happiness is our behaviour and thoughts. Our experiences only seem to affect 10% of our happiness levels and a whole 40% is down to how we deal with those life experiences.[2] And it doesn't matter whether they are positive or negative experiences. They still only affect 10% of our mood.

Bizarrely, a man whose happiness drops below his set point due to becoming paraplegic after a car accident will return back to his set point in the same amount of time as a man whose happiness goes up due to winning millions on the lottery.

Research has shown, time and time again, that massive positives such as winning a lottery will only influence our mood for 12 months, after which we just return to exactly how happy we were before we won.

And similarly, massive negatives, even something that would cause enormous despair such as the death of a child, will actually only influence our happiness levels for a year. All this is with the proviso that our thoughts and our behaviour don't change, though. Remember, of the 50% of happiness that we can control, only 10% of it is affected by our experiences, whereas learning how to better control our thoughts and our behaviour will affect 40%. If our pursuit of happiness is based solely on changing our conditions, then we won't ever become permanently happier.

If you have a low set point of happiness and then win the lottery it will lift your mood, but not permanently. Having all the money you need can give you the opportunity to learn how to be happy, but you have to take the opportunity. Giving up work may mean that you can spend more time with your family and have more time to do the things you love. It increases the chances of you never returning to your original set point of happiness ever again. But only if you know what makes you happy, because it might not be big houses and fast cars.

If you have a high set point of happiness and then lose your legs in a car accident, you are going to see a drop in your happiness levels. But if after that all you do is sit and feel sorry for yourself, then you may never return to your high set point of happiness again. Whereas accepting the disability and embracing life despite it means that you can be just as happy as you were before; it just takes a year of adjustment.

Controlling thoughts and emotions

Have you ever heard of CBT? Cognitive Behavioural Therapy (or CBT) is a form of talking therapy based on the theory that our internal dialogue is ultimately responsible for our behaviours and emotions. CBT suggests that if we can find alternative ways of thinking, then we can create a better environment that allows positive changes to happen. By improving our thoughts, we can improve our behaviours. If our previous behaviours reinforced or confirmed our thoughts and led to negative emotions, then new behaviours will reinforce our new way of thinking and create new emotions.

As an example of this process in action we'll look at Janet. Janet is 41, single and works in an office. She is competent at her job and very sweet but gets extremely nervous around her boss. He will often shout at her and she will then get upset and cry, spoiling her day. This means she avoids her boss as much as she can, often delaying giving him reports he's asked for until the last minute, which gives him more reasons to shout at her. This cycle continues until one morning before work her brain won't let her get into her car and she has a panic attack outside her front door; surprising her postman, her neighbours and a middle-aged divorced man called Jeff who is out walking his dog. Janet is signed off work by her doctor, develops a huge fear of judgement from other people and finds it impossible to ever go back to work. But it could have ended so differently if her thought processes were more appropriate.

Firstly, her boss shouts at her and it makes her cry. There's a well-trodden path in the cornfield there by the sound of it. So well trodden that she's gone from A to Z at such a speed that she didn't notice anything in between. There was an internal dialogue that went by so quickly she maybe didn't hear it. What was the subject of this unconscious inner dialogue that could cause her to become so upset, though?

It was the reason behind why her boss was shouting. Her internal voice would have said something along the lines of, "He's shouting at me because I'm so bad at my job, because I'm so useless." This would have led to an emotion that made her cry, and it's worth recognising this because a different inner dialogue would have created a better emotion. If her internal voice had said, "He's shouting at me because he's not that good a manager" or "He's having a bad day – I bet he's had an argument with his wife this morning," then there would be a different emotion and a different outcome. One of these different outcomes might eventually culminate in her leaving her house one morning to get into her car and cheerily saying "Hello" to her postman, which catches the attention of a middle-aged divorced man called Jeff walking his dog who looks up, smiles at her and makes a mental note to walk his dog down this road at this time every morning so as to catch her eye again. He does this and they eventually become great friends, fall in love and live happily ever after. The end.

That's the basis of CBT – that it's not actually what happens to us that influences us, but rather it's the way we think about those events. I remember a few years ago nipping out from one of my clinics to get some lunch from a supermarket. I parked up in one of the few spaces that were left and was in and out of the supermarket in only a few minutes. But when I got back to my car I found a woman in my way. She was bent over next to my driver's door and seemed to be looking underneath the car parked next to me. I gave a little cough to get her attention and joked, "Have you lost a pound?" She stood up and spun around in one quick, fluid motion, appearing in front of me with a scowl. "I'm looking at a scratch on my car!" she yelled. Her outburst surprised me; I'd been having a nice day up until that point and the juxtaposition between enjoying the day and her furious face scowling at me rather caught me off guard. I'm not usually at a loss for words but all I could muster in that rather odd moment was a strange stuttering relating to not being able to get in my car, whilst shuffling my feet. She became even angrier for some reason but stepped aside so as to give me room to open my car door. She stared at me, shaking her head and uttering things like "How rude!" and occasional half-finished sentences such as "You mean you're...?" and "Are you just going to...?" With my appetite quickly fading, I put my sad supermarket sandwich on the passenger seat and pulled away as quickly as I could. Even as I drove away she had one hand on her hip and the other pointing at me whilst continuing to shake her head.

I was perplexed and a little sad by the whole encounter. Someone didn't like me and I didn't know why. The drive back to my clinic wasn't too far but far enough for me to replay the interaction over and over again and feel more and more rejected with each repetition of it. It upset me, and I knew I needed to clear my head before my next client, so I decided to find an alternative way of thinking about the situation.

In Cognitive Behavioural Therapy there is a useful process called the ABC model. 'A' is the Activating Event, 'B' is the Belief and 'C' stands for Consequences. Often people think they jump from 'A' to 'C' with nothing in between. Janet, for example, sees A (her boss shouting at her) and C (making her cry), but she doesn't acknowledge the crucial role of belief. The reason Janet was upset is because it reinforced her *belief* that she was no good at her job, making her feel worthless. It was THAT that made her cry.

Using the same model, I was able to see that the reason I was upset in the car park was because I was having the wrong thoughts too.

A: The woman was angry with me.
B: My beliefs are that people have to like me
   for me to be happy.
C: I felt rejected and hurt.

I could see that I had the wrong belief. Not everyone is going to like me in life. In fact I'm quite a bouncy, effervescent sort of character that some people often find over the top and annoying, and I need to get used to that.

So, I needed to replace that belief with a new one. As with Janet, the issue was more a reflection of someone else rather than me. The woman was angry, and now that I was a little calmer I could see why. She had returned to her car to find a scratch on it and there was now a car parked next to her. Therefore, the owner of this new car (me) must have damaged hers and is a selfish idiot. Upon returning, he makes a joke about it and drives off without acknowledging what he'd done. No wonder she was angry.

By changing my belief to something more appropriate such as "She made a mistake and misjudged me", I was able to let it go and move on with the rest of my day. After all, I know I hadn't damaged her car and I know I don't need everyone to like me all the time. My self-esteem should be high enough that people can misjudge me without it changing the way I feel about myself.

It might sound like a lot of hard work to be challenging your thoughts every time you think about something that could drag you down, but remember that anything you repeat often enough will become second nature; you just need to walk a new path in the cornfield enough times for the old path to become overgrown.

One of the ways to help with negative thinking is a technique called thought stopping.

Thought stopping is a technique that originally used something such as an elastic band on your wrist to interrupt your thoughts. If you were obsessing over something, you'd pull back the elastic band, let it go and it would give you a little shock and help you to move on with your day. It's really only a step away from slapping a hysterical woman and is equally as unsuccessful at taking control over our thoughts. In fact, research has shown that having the elastic band on your wrist may even remind you of your obsessive thoughts and is likely to mean you obsess even more.[3] This is because of what's called thought rebounding. When we actively try to suppress a thought, we find that immediately afterwards we will have a substantial increase of those thoughts. It's like telling someone not to think about a pink elephant; all they'll think about is pink elephants. But if you tell someone to deliberately think about a blue goose then it's quite unlikely that they'll think about a pink elephant. In the case of emotional and mental health, trying not to think about things that would upset you actually encourages your brain to focus on it even more and so you need to take more control over where your thoughts go. This is how thought stopping should work. Instead of trying NOT to think about something you should instead deliberately think about something else.

There are always alternative thoughts to have, no matter what you're obsessing about. Some thoughts have an opposite that is more appealing and some things just need totally replacing. Clients will often talk to me about their obsessive thoughts and one that crops up a lot is the thought of someone close to them being hurt. Whether it's their children or their partner, it's common for people to obsess over the thought of a loved one being in a car accident, when instead they should be creating an expectation of them walking in the door or of hearing them pull up on the gravel drive outside. If you've been having those sorts of negative thoughts, then you probably have a very good imagination, in which case use it to your advantage. Imagine the meal you'll have together that night, the TV programmes you might watch or the conversations you might have. If you do this enough times, it soon becomes second nature and you'll find that you'll be thinking more about the things you'd like to see happen rather than the things you fear might happen.

If your negative thinking isn't something that has a specific opposite (maybe you replay an argument from earlier that day or a conversation that you wished you'd handled differently, for example), then take your mind on to anything at all, absolutely anything. Sing 'Three Blind Mice' or the theme from *Fraggle Rock*. Remember a holiday that you had when you were 12 where you saw a drunk man fall up some steps. It doesn't really matter what you end up using, provided it's something that you don't mind thinking about. Negative thoughts are too easy to focus on, probably because our brain associates them with a negative emotion, so you can't simply ignore an obsessive thought and jump straight on to something else. The original thought has way more emotional responses than its alternative, so you may need to follow this process:

EXERCISE

THOUGHT STOPPING

- As soon as you notice that you're obsessing over a thought, you need to shout, as loud as you can in your head, the word STOP! Don't shout it out for real or you'll have the neighbours knocking on your door.

- You can shout it as many times as you like or just the once. But if it's just the once, let it ring out in your mind for three or four seconds at least. STOOOOOOOOP!

- Picture something that represents the word STOP: a traffic light, a road sign, a penguin holding up a placard. It doesn't really matter what it is – you're learning to control your thoughts, and anything that can capture your attention will work fine, no matter how odd the image is.

EXERCISE

- Once you've moved your focus of attention away from the obsessive thought, you'll have more control over where it goes next. Stopping your thoughts isn't the important part of the process; you want to train yourself to have better thoughts in the first place.

- Think for a moment about what's going on. Is there an alternative belief needed?

- Can you think of something more appropriate?

- If you can't, then try remembering the theme tune to *Fraggle Rock* or *The Fresh Prince of Bel-Air*.

- Whatever you do with your thoughts, as long is it's more appropriate than what you were doing with them before, it's going to be a good distraction.

If our brain is trying to protect us or trying to keep us safe, then it will often focus on the worst-case scenario, even though, here in the 21st century, we don't have to hide in our caves from sabre-toothed tigers any more. But because we needed to be finely attuned to predators for such a long period of our prehistoric past, our brain has become hardwired to look for danger.

Now, we can call this response anything we like, but it still starts with fear. The thing is that now we have bigger frontal lobes in our brains than our early human ancestors, we can think, we can worry, and we can interpret the sensations that our brain creates throughout our bodies depending on what we have just thought about or experienced.

Our brains send a signal that says that something is different to the norm, and if it's because we know we've got an important presentation to do at work, then it manifests as anxiety. If it's because we've just come back from the vet having had our dog put to sleep then it manifests as grief. But the signals are all the same. The brain sends a message to the gut to redirect blood flow and to the adrenal glands to produce adrenaline to speed up the heart. This is often called the fight or flight response, and it doesn't make any difference whether your brain sends these signals because you're getting ready to fight for your life or getting ready for a job interview – your body reacts in the same way.

The reason for shutting off blood flow to the gut is simply because digesting your breakfast is not a priority when dealing with a threat. The oxygen carried throughout the blood is far more beneficial in the muscles instead, so you can use them for fight or flight. This is why we may feel 'butterflies' when we're nervous – the blood is being pulled out of the gut to get as much oxygen into the muscles as possible. In extreme cases, this can even make us vomit, as it does for Argentine footballer Lionel Messi. Considered to be the best player in the world and regarded by many as one of the greatest football players of all time, he has often thrown up on the pitch during a match because of his nerves. The singer Adele has clocked up more awards than her shelf can probably handle, yet she regularly suffered from anxiety attacks, and once in Brussels, she projectile-vomited on an audience member because she was so nervous.

This physiological response to stress is quite normal, perhaps a little extreme in these examples but still normal nonetheless. We are all going to experience it to some varying degree most days and understanding it is vital, in order to live a happy life.

One of the best ways of learning how to control our emotions is to learn how to breathe efficiently. After all, the reason for this physiological change in the body is due to an increased demand for oxygen. So breathe. Go on take a deep breath, and get as much air into your lungs as you can. Did you do it? Did you take a deep breath? Or did you actually take a shallow breath?

If you've ever had singing lessons or played a wind instrument or if you've ever gone to a yoga class, then you may already know how to breathe efficiently. The mistake that people tend to make is that when they breathe in they pull their stomach in and puff their chest out to try and expand their lungs. But the rib cage is in the way and so the lungs can't expand. It gives the impression that the lungs are full, but actually they're probably still half empty. This causes two things to happen, to make up for the fact that there is not enough oxygen circulating in the blood. Firstly, adrenaline is released to speed up the heart and direct what little oxygen is in the blood around the body as fast as possible, and secondly, breathing speeds up to try and get even more oxygen in. This leads to a feeling of breathlessness, which can sometimes make us panic. That panic gives our brain even more reason to think there's a threat, and so it creates an even greater demand for oxygen, sending the body into a panic attack spiral. Which is probably the reason why Adele projectile-vomited onto one of her fans in Brussels that day. Here is a guide to help regulate your breathing to get as much oxygen circulating as possible:

EXERCISE

DIAPHRAGMATIC BREATHING

- Place one hand on your chest and the other on your stomach.

- Allow your shoulders to relax and hang a little more loosely.

- Push your stomach out slightly.

- Breathe in and push your stomach out a little more as you do so (I don't care if it makes you feel fat; it's also going to make you feel calmer).

- Ensure that the hand that's on your chest doesn't really move that much.

- As you breathe in, count to three.

- Hold your breath and count to three.

- Breathe out slowly for the count of six.

- Repeat another two or three times.

This way of breathing will give your body a huge boost of oxygen, which prevents the need for adrenaline, slows down the heart and sends a little signal to your brain that says, "Chill out, we're all right. The sabre-toothed tiger must have gone." Some people find it easier to learn this while lying on their back, so if you're struggling with this, maybe go and have a lie down as you practise it. Soon you'll be able to breathe this way while driving, talking or just falling asleep.

It might seem like a simple technique to help calm you down, but as an actor I've found this invaluable when on stage and probably couldn't get through a play without it. But don't just wait until you're anxious about something. The best way to get good at anything is to do it so often that it becomes second nature. That way when you do need to calm yourself down a bit because you're angry or frustrated, it will be much easier. So do it every hour. Get into a habit that once every hour you turn your thoughts to your breathing, and within a few weeks it will become much easier to keep calm in stressful situations and deal with any changes that you make in life.

Visualisation

Once you have some control over your thoughts and your emotions, you can then start using your brain more effectively and begin steering your thoughts in a more positive direction.

Positive thinking is a bit of an overused phrase and often conjures up ideas of mantras such as Émile Coué's famous "Every day, in every way, I am getting better and better", even though that example is more often quoted in satire than anywhere else. But can such a mantra really help? It can to a certain degree, I think. After all, the brain can't distinguish fact from fiction, which I'll come back to shortly. Either way, I certainly don't recommend doing the opposite, and reciting "Every day, in every way, I am getting crapper and crapper".

But we can't just rely on positive thinking. If deep down we know something not to be true then these sorts of statements won't have much of an effect, and may in fact make us feel worse when the effort we put in seems futile. Plenty of research has demonstrated the counter-intuitive negative effects of thinking about achieving your goals, and yet so many self-help books will suggest spending time doing just that. "If you can see it, you can be it!" isn't all it's cracked up to be.

Let me tell you why. I mentioned that the brain doesn't know the difference between fact and fiction. You've probably experienced evidence of that many times. If you've ever watched *You've Been Framed* and cringed when a man has crunched his testicles painfully onto the frame of his bicycle then you know what I mean. Similarly when my son was young, he would often come home with a note from his teacher asking the parents to please check their child's hair for head lice. Now, I never had head lice as a child and have no experience of how it would feel, but I can imagine it. And because I can imagine how it would feel, my scalp is being sent signals from my brain as if I do have head lice. Even writing this now is making my head itch. Yours might even be starting to itch a little now too, just by thinking about the idea of having head lice.

What's happening here is that when you think about

something happening, your brain fires off neurons as if it's happening for real. Now, this can be a good thing and it can also be a pain in the backside.

If you think about taking the dog for a walk with a cheery smile on your face, then, more than likely, that's what will happen.

Think about dropping your pint on the way back from the bar and, guess what? It'll probably happen. I remember once talking about this with a police officer who had recently undertaken an advanced driving course. He told me that one of the skills he had to master was driving at speed, and so he had to practise weaving in and out of a row of cones. At first he was ploughing through them, knocking them all down, time after time. The instructor asked him where his focus of attention was and he said that it was the cones, obviously. So the instructor suggested he shift his attention away from the cones and instead focus his attention onto the spaces in between them. After all that's where he wants the car to be. Doing this he was able to weave through the cones quite easily and pass his test.

So it makes sense to spend your time thinking about all the things that you want to see happen, doesn't it?

Well, maybe not always.

What if you want to lose weight, you want to become fitter and healthier. Imagining being slimmer obviously won't suddenly make it happen or even motivate you to do anything about your current weight, as I'll explain below. As for the phrase "If you can see it, you can be it!", I agree that when it comes to making changes in life every decision you make starts in your mind. But ONLY daydreaming about it? No.

In fact what people often find is that the excitement of

thinking about their desired end result can actually prevent them from getting started in the first place.

An example of this in action was in a study at the University of California.[4]

A group of students were asked to spend a few minutes each day visualising themselves getting a high mark on their imminent mid-term exams. They were asked to 'form a clear image in their mind's eye and imagine how great it would feel to get a high mark'.

They were also asked to make a note of the number of hours they studied each day, and their final marks were compared to a control group of students, who just carried on as usual and were not asked to visualise anything.

The visualisation exercise was only for a few minutes, but it had quite a significant effect on the students' behaviour. Those students who had spent time imagining their desired end result studied less and got lower marks in their exam. It had the exact opposite effect to what they wanted.

Instead of encouraging them to study, what the visualisation exercise created was false confidence. It may have made them feel positive about their abilities, but did not actually help them to achieve a high mark. Confidence is only going to help you if you already know your stuff in the first place. But false confidence is going to mean you think you know more than you actually do.

The same thing happened in another part of the study, in which students were asked to imagine having their perfect career. The results showed that the more they daydreamed about it, the less work they put into actually making it happen. Following the students up after two years revealed that this group hadn't applied for as many jobs as other students had and the jobs that they had ended up with involved significantly lower starting salaries.

When it comes to using your imagination to encourage you, it's obvious that just imagining the result is much easier than actually making it happen.

It's much easier to dream your life than to live your dream. So it's important to always focus on the steps in between, not just the end result. This is called process visualisation (as opposed to outcome visualisation) and combining the two is vital in order to get the best out of the exercise. If you have a goal in mind – whether it's to lose weight, run a half marathon, change your job or even fall in love, this is how to do it:

EXERCISE

PROCESS VISUALISATION

- Set 15 minutes to one side and either lie on your bed or sit comfortably somewhere with your eyes closed.

- Take a few deep breaths to slow your body down a little; this will help you to focus your attention on your thoughts.

- Start off by simply thinking about the desired outcome. If it's to become fitter, think about the energy level you want, the way your clothes fit you better or the way you look in a mirror.

- Begin to immerse yourself in the daydream, so you're not just thinking about that end result but almost playing a story in your mind and imagining conversations or specific outcomes. EXAMPLE: If your goal is to find a job, imagine getting dressed on your first day and follow the daydream along throughout your day. Imagine yourself introducing yourself and shaking hands with new colleagues.
EXAMPLE: Weight loss. Imagine a future where you've achieved your goal and you're at your ideal weight, shape or size. Imagine friends congratulating you and telling you how good you

EXERCISE

look. Think about how it would feel to be fitter and healthier. Visualise some simple, everyday things becoming easier, such as climbing stairs or chasing your children around a park.

- Bear in mind that visualisation is not just about 'seeing' things in your mind though. Many people even say that they find it impossible to imagine what something would look like and instead they talk about how an experience would feel, sound or even smell. So don't worry if when doing this you find yourself using different senses to 'picture' something, it just means that your best sense isn't visual.

- Now that you've identified a goal and used outcome visualisation to imagine the end result, it's time to hone your visualisation skills with the most important part of the exercise: process visualisation. Unless your end goal is amazingly small it will have steps that lead you to it and this is where the majority of your focus needs to be. EXAMPLE: If you want to lose weight, think about how you'll do it; think about the exercises that you'll be doing and the healthier choices you'll be making. Maybe it starts in the planning of meals before you go to the supermarket. EXAMPLE: If you want a great career, think about

EXERCISE

the phone calls you'll be making, the work you're going to put into it and the excitement that doing THAT will create, not just the excitement of already having the job.

- Next, imagine the hurdles, the setbacks, the things that could prevent you from succeeding. Thinking about how things could go wrong might not sound like a great plan, but bear with me, because negative thinking is not all doom and gloom. You are better prepared to deal with any obstacles you might face if you've already rehearsed how you would deal with them. So, if your goal is to eat healthier, what's stopping you? Is it your partner making you a cup of tea at 10pm and bringing in a packet of biscuits with it? If so, imagine how you're going to handle that situation better. Go into some finer details by imagining how you would 'feel' about handling it better, the pride in knowing that you feel comfortable declining an unhealthy snack.
EXAMPLE: If your goal is to finish a degree, what are the obstructions? Imagine something that makes it difficult for you to work and see how you can work around it. Imagine yourself turning down a social event; after all you can't attend everything someone invites you to, and

EXERCISE

imagine that you handle it well without any fear of missing out.

EXAMPLE: Quitting smoking. Maybe imagine a social event with a friend who smokes and they offer you a cigarette. Step into that scene in your mind and imagine how you'd handle it if they tease you. If you smoke when stressed then get prepared for that by imagining a situation that puts you under pressure. See yourself dealing with it better, perhaps walking away for a few moments and taking some deep breaths before carrying on as a non-smoker.

• If visualisation is new to you, then be patient, because it might take a bit of practice before you can immerse yourself into your imagination. A great time to do this is in bed before you fall asleep. If, two or three times per week, you go to bed 15 minutes earlier and practise visualisation, you'll find that in a short time you'll probably be able to do it anywhere, maybe even with your eyes open while standing in a bus queue. Your expectations of the future are based on your experiences from the past. By creating more desirable experiences, even imaginary ones, you will create some better expectations that lead you to succeeding. That's how much of an effect our daydreams have on our lives, so use them to your advantage.

Liu Shikun

Liu Shikun was born near Beijing, China, in 1939. His father was a trained singer who encouraged his son from a very early age to follow in his footsteps, and by three years old, Shikun was already playing the piano. "I sat on my father's knees..." he says "...because I couldn't reach the keyboard."

His father taught him to memorise classical music by humming it, and at five years old the young Shikun could hum entire Beethoven symphonies; and he was performing piano in public before he was six.

Great things were expected of him and so, at 12 years old, he was enrolled in a music college for the musically gifted. By 17 he had become skilled enough to take part in international competitions, and was (rather oddly) given a lock of Hungarian composer Franz Liszt's hair after winning two prizes at the Liszt International Piano Competition in Hungary in 1956.

Shikun soon became one of China's premier concert performers. Until 1966 that was, with the advent of Mao Zedong's Cultural Revolution. In order to achieve his goal of preserving 'true' Communist ideology by purging remnants of capitalist elements from Chinese society, thousands of artists, writers and musicians were imprisoned and classical music was made illegal. Shikun was sadly arrested and jailed for six years.

During those six years, Shikun had nothing to do and had no interaction with anyone other than prison guards who would occasionally beat him.

With nothing to do and no piano to play, Shikun went to the only place he could go, his imagination. Although quite a private man, he has given a few interviews over the years. One of his first was to *People* magazine, seven years after his release in 1979. He talked about how he would sit in his cell, day after day, night after night and practised playing his favourite concertos in his mind. He'd walk on stage, nod to his audience and with a flick of the tails of his jacket he'd sit at a Steinway piano and begin. The Piano Concerto No. 1 in B flat minor, Op. 23, was composed by Pyotr Ilyich Tchaikovsky in 1875 and played by Liu Shikun every day in his head for six years.

Every day he gave a stirring performance of Franz Liszt's Piano Concerto No. 1 in E flat major to an adoring audience, with a display of manic intensity as the orchestra excitedly attempted to keep up with the breakneck speed of his piano playing.

Shikun didn't just simply remember the music; he experienced it. He felt the warmth of the lights and the coolness of the piano keys. He soaked up the scent of a 1914 Steinway, a subtle fragrance of musky old wood and polish, before looking up at his conductor on his podium. Watching and listening for him to tap his baton against his music stand. Feeling a little burst of excitement when he did as his accompanying orchestra burst into life.

He wrote new pieces of music, even a whole concerto despite having no pen or paper to write it down. He recorded it in his mind every day and played it over and over again, locking it in his memory.

Shikun experienced this every single day of his imprisonment, whether or not his arms were damaged from the beatings. In his mind he was skilled, healthy and versatile. Upon his release from prison he was soon playing again, because the Chinese government were desperate to prove that their leading pianist was still alive and quash the rumours that he had been killed or had his hands cut off. He played as well as he had ever played, as if he had kept up with the hours and hours of constant practice that piano virtuosos usually require to maintain their expertise, despite not having seen a real piano for six years.

Such is the power of our imagination – an often undervalued and underused ability that we all possess. An ability that with practice becomes a skill that can steer us towards success or towards failure, depending on what we do with it.

Optimism

So how does understanding the role of our imagination make us happier? After all we can't just visualise ourselves into being happy can we? Maybe not, but recognising that our personality isn't set in stone, that we have the capacity to change, can give us hope and create optimism, even if your genetic set point of happiness is low.

In the same way that someone with an inherited heart condition needs to keep healthy by eating sensibly and exercising regularly, someone with a low happiness set point can develop attitudes and behaviours that will lift it to that of someone with a high set point.

In order to become more of an optimist, ask yourself this question. Do you control your destiny or does your destiny control you?

The extent to which people believe that they have control over their own lives is what's referred to in psychology as the 'locus of control'. Someone with a very external locus of control tends to believe that their own behaviour doesn't matter a great deal and that any rewards in life are generally outside of their control. They are less likely to apply for a promotion because they believe that the successful candidate has already been chosen, and they are less likely to vote in an election because they feel that their vote won't affect the outcome.

Those who have an internal locus of control and don't think that luck or chance plays a huge part in determining what happens in their life are generally happier. They are less likely to see themselves as a victim and more likely to learn from their mistakes. They are more likely to be optimistic because they can easily imagine the outcomes that they want in life and the steps they need to take.

But they can become too optimistic, which blinds them to potential pitfalls and causes them to fall at the first hurdle. Having a very high internal locus of control can mean we come down to earth with a real bump, and because we consider ourselves ultimately in control then we've only got ourselves to blame. That's going to hurt.

So although it's generally accepted that having an internal locus of control is better for us, we also need to be realists. After all, we can't control everything. The American theologian Reinhold Niebuhr summed it up with his famous Serenity Prayer, which was adopted and popularised by Alcoholics Anonymous and other twelve-step programmes. It is often shortened to simply:

"Grant me the serenity to accept the things I
cannot change,
The courage to change the things I can,
And wisdom to know the difference."

All the optimism in the world makes no difference if you carry around a belief that everything is your responsibility. I was chatting with a colleague at a psychotherapy conference recently and they were talking about how they had struggled when a client of theirs had committed suicide. They told me how they had sensed that something wasn't quite right about them in their last session, and they wished they had dealt with them differently that day. Yet, unless the client was to have come right out and said what they were planning, there was no way of actually knowing and preventing them from doing it. This is what happens when your locus of control is too internal – you feel more responsible than you should. It is why some colleagues of mine burn out if they have more than three or four clients on their books at a time, while some can handle dozens without a problem.

One of the interesting and rather unexpected results from research into the benefits of visualisation came out of the University of Pennsylvania, and was undertaken by Professor Gabriele Oettingen. What she and her team discovered was the surprising benefit of negative thinking as well as positive thinking. It turns out that you're more likely to achieve the things you want in life if you not only have the end result in your mind and the steps that will take you to it but also a realistic view of the hurdles you could face. Thinking about the worst-case scenario doesn't sound very optimistic and is often called 'catastrophising', but when used in the right way it can actually be beneficial. What psychologists suggest is that if you imagine your problems and setbacks but then continue the fantasy onward in time you will find it often works out OK in the end. The idea that despite the setback, we all live happily ever after anyway.

If you find yourself catastrophising, ask yourself, "And then what?" For example if you're constantly doubting your skills at work and you're worried about being given a verbal warning, ask yourself, "And then what?" It could be that this leads to the HR department arranging some useful training for you. But it could mean that your anxiety rises, your confidence drops even lower and you end up with a written warning. You could play the fantasy out even further and think that you could lose your job! Lose your house! What will happen to your children?! This is catastrophising. But still ask yourself, "And then what?" What would you have to do if you lost your job and your house? Move in with a family member for a time while the local authority arranged a house for you? It might be unpleasant, but it's not the end of the world.

Often it's the fear of the worst-case scenario that causes us anxiety, but if you can begin to understand that you're more resilient than you think – that you can handle being let down or disappointed and still live happily ever after – then it becomes easier to handle the 'mountain out of a mole hill' type of thinking.

On a smaller scale, when learning to improve anything in your life, you also need to take into account the things you might struggle with the most. What are your 'buts'?

"I would look for another job, but..."

"I would exercise more, but..."

"I would join a community group, but..."

Find out what your 'buts' are and then argue with yourself. We all have many 'parts' to our personality that share our internal monologue in our mind, a part that wants to do this and a part that wants to do that. Turn them into dialogue if you have to and begin to encourage yourself. Sometimes in order to be an optimist, you have to listen to the pessimist in you as well. The pessimist is just trying to protect you from getting hurt, from disappointment, but there will be alternative ways of thinking about a situation. Look for evidence that opposes your inner pessimist, even if it feels fake to do so at first, because it will become habitual. Doing it over and over again soon means that it's easier to think positively. It ingrains more and more into your personality and the optimistic realist becomes the dominant voice in your head. If the pessimist in you is quite strong, remember one thing: there's no point in being a pessimist; it wouldn't work anyway.

Journalling

In learning to be happier, you might need to stretch your comfort zone a little bit, and do things that you might normally find a little anxiety-provoking. The most important thing to recognise is that you are capable of change. Let me say that again but a bit louder. YOU ARE CAPABLE OF CHANGE! Your personality may have some genetic connection, but that doesn't mean that it's set in stone; you aren't stuck.

Making changes to the way that you think and behave is likely to unnerve you, but this is nothing more than the fight or flight response in action. So practise those diaphragmatic breathing exercises to counteract it, and seriously consider the idea of writing a journal.

Keeping a personal journal is a great way of helping to gain a better perspective on things. Research has even shown it to have similar benefits to counselling.[5]

But it needs to be done properly. Writing a journal shouldn't be about wallowing in self-pity. It should be a tool to help you to see alternative ways of thinking, feeling and behaving. A way of looking back over what you've written so you can see the changes in your attitude over time. Doing this will create a wonderful domino effect that will make you even more optimistic for the future.

So grab a notepad and a pencil and get writing. It doesn't need to be perfect. The grammar and spelling can be all over the place and it doesn't need to be creative. But it's important to remember what I said earlier about our beliefs or thoughts sitting between events we experience and their emotional consequences.

If you're going to write about something that happened that day which made you unhappy, also write about the thoughts you had that allowed the unhappy feeling. Write about how you'd prefer to think and feel if it were to happen again.

If you've ever written an angry email or a text message to someone but then not sent it, then you've used this process before. You can write the message and feel a bit better even though they will never read what you wanted to say to them.

Writing in a journal can be a bit like that. Moving your thoughts and emotions from your head onto paper helps you to separate yourself from them and helps you to feel calmer and less stressed. Using an electronic device doesn't seem to have quite the same effect for a lot of people, though. Sure, it's more private and if that's more important to you because you live in a shared flat full of nosey folk, then it might be better to use an app or just a text document on a password-protected computer. One very easy way of keeping an electronic journal is to set up a new email address, using something like Gmail. That way you can simply email your thoughts to it knowing that no one will be able to log into it to read them. You can periodically log in yourself and read through past messages and gain insight and hopefully see how far you've come. Having said that, nothing can beat using a simple notebook because it allows you to simply dump everything that's in your head without being able to edit it afterwards. The whole idea of this process is to give you a space to let your thoughts flow easily, and knowing that you can edit out bits or change it to make it perfect isn't helpful. If you've never done anything like it before then it might feel a bit weird to you, but then so did wearing underwear but you soon got used to it (I hope).

If you are 100% absolutely dead-set against the idea of a journal then you're going to have to work a bit harder. But you can still gain benefits from the process. The best alternative is probably to use a voice recorder app on your phone and go for a walk for ten minutes. Pretend you're talking to a friend and offload to them, talk about your day, your life and your insecurities. Talk about your goals and the steps you'll need to take to reach them.

If you ever get stuck about something to journal about, there are a few prompts at the end of each chapter of this book.

EXERCISE

JOURNALLING STARTING BLOCKS

- Start with the date!
  If you're writing your journal by hand, remember to date your entry. This way you can see exactly where you were in life at the time and it can also help you to see where the gaps are.

- So, what do you want to write about?
  If you're not sure, ask yourself a few questions. How do you feel right now? What's on your mind? Actually write the words "Today I feel..." or "I want..." and see what comes next.

- Write quickly.
  If you keep on going, then your inner critic can't get in the way of the process by censoring you.

- Pick some specific days to write and stick to them – two or three days per week would be fine. Doing it every day would be amazing, and depending on what's going on in your life that may well be appropriate. But for most people more than three times per week might be a little over the top. Just find a topic that you want to write about and have a brain dump for 15 minutes.

EXERCISE

- There are no rules.
  Everyone may do this differently, so just do it in a
  way that works for you.

- Be honest.
  Many things that are on your mind would make
  you feel bad if you were to say them in public,
  but your journal isn't public. There might be
  things you need to write about that would make
  you feel guilty just for thinking them, but that's
  fine. Accept it and even write about the emotions
  that the journalling process brings up for you. If
  you ever hesitate over whether or not something
  needs to be written about, then that means it
  probably does.

- Reflect.
  Go back and re-read previous entries from time
  to time and notice how time and experience can
  change how you think and feel about what you
  wrote about. It will help you to see how you've
  developed and move you in a positive direction.

The routine of keeping a journal is almost as important as the brain dump itself. It will help you to create some sense of order in your life, even if it often feels like it's in chaos. According to social psychologist Roy F. Baumeister, who researched willpower and self-regulation at Florida State University, adding new habits into your life actually strengthens your willpower, which means that other difficult things become easier too.[6] So you may find that keeping a journal reduces your inclination to snap at someone at work, even though you've told them a thousand times exactly where the staples are kept.

But primarily, writing in a journal will help you to understand yourself better. It will show you more about what really makes you tick. It will help you to challenge and change the inner dialogue in your mind by showing you any insecurities and fears in a safe and non-judgemental way. And it will help you to answer that all-important question: What is happiness to you?

And when you figure that out, I wonder if it will be the presence of something good? Or the absence of something bad?

But maybe it will end up being a mixture of both of them.

The Happy Mix

Last spring, while relaxing and watching my son bounce on a trampoline in the garden, my wife said to me, "If it was always like this, people would be a lot happier."

My instincts were to concur, and I started to nod my head in agreement before stepping back and thinking about her statement first.

If there is a correlation between the sun and happiness, then the happiest countries in the world would also be the ones that have the most sunshine. But, as I found out later, that's not the case.

According to the World Happiness Report undertaken by Gallup[7] the top five happy countries are Norway, Denmark, Iceland, Switzerland and Finland. One thousand people from each of the 150 countries involved in the research were interviewed and asked the following question:

"Please imagine a ladder with steps numbered from zero at the bottom to ten at the top. Suppose we say that the top of the ladder represents the best possible life for you, and the bottom of the ladder represents the worst possible life for you. On which step of the ladder would you say you personally feel you stand at this time, assuming that the higher the step the better you feel about your life, and the lower the step the worse you feel about it? Which step comes closest to the way you feel?"

This question is asked once per year and the answers are combined with the previous two years' answers to work out an average for each country.

But why are Norway, Denmark, Iceland, Switzerland and Finland at the top? Geographically they are all quite close and so may well have similar weather, but they do not have the most sunshine in the world, not by a long way.

The countries with the most sunshine are Egypt and Sudan and they are right down towards the very bottom of the happiness chart.

So, if the sun doesn't seem to make us any happier at all,

why on that lovely Sunday afternoon sitting with my wife drinking coffee and staring out of the window watching my son bounce on his trampoline did we both think that if life was always like this then everyone would be happy?

Maybe it was because it was the first sunny weekend of the year. Or maybe it wasn't the nice day by itself that made us happier – perhaps the absence of a nice day prior to then had an impact.

It was the cold and THEN the warmth.

It was the rain and THEN the sunshine.

Going back to the World Happiness Report, the bottom countries are Syria, Tanzania, Burundi and Central African Republic.

They all get alot of sunshine but they also have alot of restrictions on freedom of expression and abuses of human rights, which are things that Western Europe doesn't have as many concerns over.

I propose that, on its own, the sunshine does nothing to improve our happiness levels. If it was always sunny then we would easily become accustomed to it and it would stop having any effect on us. The reason why that weekend of good weather in early spring last year made everyone so happy was the contrast with how it HAD been.

How can we enjoy the sunshine if we didn't first have to deal with the grey drizzle of an English February?

How can we feel happy if we didn't at some point feel miserable?

We need to recognise that we can't be happy all the time, otherwise we just normalise that too. In order to live a happy life we need to be unhappy at some point, so that we can then enjoy life more when it lifts.

Be true to who you are!

If you're feeling miserable, be miserable!

Don't put huge pressure on yourself to become happier as it will only make you feel as if everybody else has got a perfect life and you're in some way broken.

Happiness isn't a thing. It's a process, a journey. And throughout that journey there will be times when you are going to feel dark, and you may have to work quite hard to see any light in your day.

In short, happiness doesn't actually show us how to be happy. Sadness does.

And the pursuit of happiness has to involve us not being happy in the first place.

Backfire

When I was first approached by the publishing company to write this book, I was asked which of my podcast topics tended to be the most popular. So I ploughed through the podcast statistics looking for any correlation between episode titles and popularity. What I found was that anything with the word 'happy' or 'happiness' in it tended to be a lot more popular than any other topic. To write about anything else seemed daft then. I need to give you what you're asking for, don't I?

I spent quite a while ruminating over this question, even though the decision was clearly being made for me by my podcast listeners. I was concerned that the social pressure to be happy was driving their decision to download those specific podcast episodes, rather than their own genuine need to be any happier.

It reminded me of the healthy-sized women who often come to my clinic asking for advice on weight loss. In the same way that society seems to expect everyone to be physically perfect, there is a growing trend for everyone to be emotionally and psychologically perfect too. Well-meaning therapists and authors regularly emphasise the importance of being happy, and I can understand why. Happy people have better friendships, are viewed as more likeable, get better-quality sleep and have a better immune system. Why would someone not want to seek out happiness and miss out on these amazing benefits?

Well, negative emotions are valuable and to think you can never experience them is totally unrealistic. I don't mean to sound cheesy but life really is a rollercoaster, with great highs and extreme lows, and as long as you keep your eyes open throughout the whole ride, you'll find that it was worth it.

Be open to the possibility that you bought this book and you don't actually need it. It's not unrealistic to think that in stopping trying to be happy, you can find that you're happy enough already. Paradoxically, it could be that the only reason for you being unhappy is your relentless attempt at trying not to be. There have been quite a few studies[8] over the years to determine whether *seeking* happiness can actually make people feel less happy than they would if they hadn't bothered, and it's not good news for all you happiness worshippers out there. In one of the studies, participants read one of two fake newspaper articles that either commended the importance of happiness or the importance of making accurate judgements. Then they were randomly assigned to watch either a happy or a sad two-minute film clip to induce emotion. The happy film showed a female figure skater winning a gold medal, the crowd's happy reactions and her coach celebrating with her. The sad film clip showed a happy couple in love spending a night out dancing, before the wife suddenly dies and it ended with the husband having to go home to an empty house. Everyone then had their emotional state tested and were asked some random questions about how the clips made them feel. When you study the results, you can see that the people who had read the fake newspaper article about the importance of happiness actually experienced greater levels of disappointment in how they felt about the positive film. They were not disappointed with the film itself, but they felt they should have enjoyed it more.

So, if we're all primed to value happiness, then we can actually become less appreciative of the positive events in our life, rather than enjoy life more.

I propose that to be truly happy we need to have a better grasp on all of our emotions, not just the positive ones. We have a wide spectrum of emotions and many different words for them, but they're all based upon the fight or flight response and they induce the same chemical and physiological changes in our body. The same nervousness in the gut, the same squirt of adrenaline into the bloodstream that bumps our heart a bit (or a lot) is the same for feeling guilty as it is for feeling angry. Two people queuing for a rollercoaster could be feeling the exact same sensations within their body, yet one person calls it fear and the other calls it excitement.

Understanding our emotions will lead to acceptance of them, and in accepting our emotions, we can then move on from them. If we don't know why we feel the way we feel, then we can easily become fearful of our emotions. Which is in itself an emotion, which we then begin to fear, and before we know it we're throwing chairs through our office window or having a panic attack in the corner.

Our brains are very clever and complex machines and can be taught to differentiate between the slightest of variances in sounds and colours, but you have to have practised experiencing them to notice the differences. I'm not particularly musical; I can bash out the main riffs from 'Smoke On The Water' and 'Iron Man' on a guitar, but I can't tell the difference between an F and an Fsus4 (F suspended fourth) chord, yet to more experienced players, they sound completely different.

The Himba tribe of northern Namibia literally see the world in a different way to everyone else. While the English language has 11 separate colour categories of red, orange, yellow, green, blue, purple, pink, brown, grey, black and white, the Himba have just five. 'Serandu' is a colour that groups together what we might think of as a shade of red, brown, orange and some yellows. 'Dambu' includes green, another red shade, beige and more shades of yellow. 'Zuzu' is used to describe the darker shades of all colours dark red, dark blue and black. 'Vapa' is the word for both light yellow and white and 'Buru' is used to describe both green and blue.

To them blue and green are not just the same word though, but they actually look the same too. The Himba find it very hard to see the difference between two coloured squares that look totally different to everyone else. The reason for this is because their environment has fewer colours for them to experience, so their brains haven't made the connections for them to perceive any difference. Except for the colour red that is. Because the Himba use different words for different reds, they can spot the slightest difference between two shades that look exactly the same to you and me.

Your brain will learn whatever you teach it if you practise, and the only way to practise understanding your emotions is to actually experience them, not shut them away and pretend they don't exist. Sure, take a few deep breaths and let the emotions dissolve, but don't pretend they weren't there. If you can't tell the difference between feeling lonely and feeling angry, then reconnecting with old friends or making new ones won't be your priority when it could be exactly what you need.

If you do something wrong but you're unable to differentiate guilt from shame, then instead of putting it right, you're going to want to hide away and make it worse.

In the days following the 9/11 attacks in New York, dozens of news reporters ran through the streets, even before the dust had really settled, desperate for a reaction from the public so as to give them some personal content in their news articles. One person said, "My first reaction was terrible sadness but then came anger, because I couldn't do anything with the sadness." A second person said, "I felt a bunch of things I couldn't put my finger on, maybe anger, confusion, fear. I just felt bad." Which of the two people are more likely to overcome their emotions and get on with their lives? It's easily the first person. Having the emotional expertise to represent emotions in specific terms allows us to feel more than simply just 'good' or 'bad'.

Research findings from multiple studies over the years has shown that being able to clearly identify what you're feeling in times of stress means we are less likely to be overwhelmed in difficult situations.[9] Dr. Lisa Feldman Barrett, Professor of Psychology at Boston College, Massachusetts, noticed that children who are able to identify, understand, and label their emotions effectively have fewer trips to their GP, are less likely to display violent behaviour, and are at a lower risk of developing drug and alcohol problems. They have better social skills, display stronger leadership qualities, and even do better in their exams. Because of this, emotional literacy has become a central component of educational reforms over the last few years. But just because we've left school, it doesn't mean we're not capable of learning something; as adults we can still learn about this stuff. I often see clients who suffer with chronic pain. Learning the difference between discomfort and distress means that the pain can still be there but it doesn't bother them so much. There is a physical discomfort, but not an emotional distress.

Emotional literacy is vital to us all; if you don't know the word for the feeling that you're experiencing, then it's just 'bad' rather than 'guilty', 'bored' or 'impatient'. If you don't know what it is, then you can't put it right. English is a mongrel language, drawing influences from all over the world over thousands of years, and yet still there are emotions that exist in other languages that don't exist in English. 'Schadenfreude', for example, a German word for the pleasure we can derive from the misfortune of others. 'Greng-jai' is a Thai word for feeling uncomfortable that someone goes out of their way to help you. 'Hygge' is the Danish word for experiencing pleasure in the simpler things in life. Then there are the English words that aren't very well known. 'Alysm' is the frustrated feeling of restlessness that comes from being ill. 'Shivviness' is an old Yorkshire word for the uncomfortable feeling you get when a label on some new underwear is scratching you. 'Huckmuck' is an old English dialect word for the uneasy feeling caused by things being out of place after tidying up, and is still sometimes used in Dorset to mean slovenly.

Aside from the underused words, there are plenty of words that you already have an awareness of that will help you to match your emotions to the right concepts. If someone talks over you in a meeting, do you feel offended, mocked or inferior? If someone forgets your birthday, are you feeling insignificant, rejected or ignored? If you don't feel educated enough to understand then try reading more, listening to different radio stations, watching different TV shows. Allow alternative ways of experiencing the world to become normal to you. Before long you'll be able to accept your emotions for what they are, and your brain will send a signal that your expectations were not met and something's not right. Whether that's something you can control or something that you can't, the answer is almost always to simply take a deep breath and move on.

Journal Suggestions

1. If your older self could travel back in time, what would they say you did that helped you overcome your problems?

2. Is there something that you wish others knew about you?

3. Write a list of questions to which you need answers to.

4. Are there any words you need to hear from someone now?

5. Are there any words you needed to hear from someone in the past?

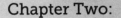

Chapter Two:

Can You Buy Happiness?

The Psychology Of Money

If you go back far enough in human history the concept of money doesn't really exist. Long ago, communities worked together more closely and if one man was good at building roofs and another man was great at making spears, then both families got mammoth for dinner and neither got wet when it rained. However, a bartering system doesn't work that well when society gets larger. One roof might equal 200 spears, but how many spears does a roofer really need? He may be able to swap them for some axes with another toolmaker, but in the meantime, where the heck is he going to keep all these sodding spears? So, sometime around 1100 BC., the Chinese had the great idea of making tiny bronze replica tools and weapons to barter with. Except that people were plunging their hands into their pouches and impaling them on the tiny tools within, and nobody really wants that. And so, over time, these mini spades and daggers were abandoned for the rather less dangerous shape of a circle, and the first coins were created. These coins were much easier to carry around, much easier to swap roofing services with and much easier to covet.

Very soon, our greedy desire for a large quantity of these coins, the paper notes that replaced them and finally the balance on our bank statements, has meant that if you ask people what one thing they would change in their life to guarantee a boost in their happiness, a huge majority will say "More money".

Yet, if you ask them "Does more money make you happier?", those same people will quote well-meaning Facebook poster quotes about true happiness coming from the inside, not the outside. So we know intellectually that more money doesn't necessarily equal a happier life for everyone, yet, at the same time, we feel that we must be the exception to the rule.

The reason for this is that for most cultures, money has begun to replace everything from our prehistoric past that signified safety. No longer do we need to worry about whether there'll be healthy crops in the lower field this year, because we can just nip to the supermarket for our Pot Noodles. So, instead, our instincts encourage us towards other ways of ensuring that we are safe, which will, by extension, make us happy.

One of the strangest ways that this phenomenon shows itself is in our deep instinct to be liked and accepted.

In our ancient past, it was a very dangerous thing indeed to be alone. If we're part of a herd of others, then when the sabre-toothed tiger attacks, there's a stronger chance they'll pick off someone else (after all, they can only grab one), so we feel safer. But if it's just us standing in a field picking our nose, staring at the clouds, then we're tiger food in no time at all. Safety in numbers, you see.

Even in our recent history, criminals were banished from their village for crimes they had committed. Shunned by everyone, they would be forced to wander the countryside in solitude until a pack of wolves would descend or they starved to death.

All these years later, with money replacing safety, we find that the more financially secure we sense we are, the less we feel the need to be in a herd or to be liked and accepted by others. It becomes safer to be rejected by someone, and we begin to care less what people think of us, because we are more self-reliant. We don't need any help from anyone to kill a woolly mammoth or put a roof on our home, and it really doesn't matter if we never see another human being again.

So what started out as a great way of boosting self-esteem could easily turn against us, as we can become selfish hermits rattling around in big houses with no one to share any of it with because we've pushed everyone away.

Over the years, various studies have been undertaken that show that wealth seems to isolate us; we end up prioritising our own goals over the needs of others and we see ourselves as vastly more important. When giving people a piece of paper and simply asking them to draw a circle to represent themselves, there is a direct correlation with their wealth and the size of the circle they draw.

You can easily replicate studies that have shown this effect by deliberately leaving it a little late to make it obvious to drivers that you want to cross at a zebra crossing. A series of studies conducted by psychologists at the University of California and the University of Toronto[10] found that the more expensive the car, the less likely they are to stop for you, even if you've been waiting patiently for them to stop. When this study was undertaken in Los Angeles, where it is against the law not to stop for pedestrians (but is a place with a high number of very wealthy drivers), they found that half of all drivers of very expensive cars happily broke the law. As a contrast, drivers of very inexpensive cars ALL stopped. Every single one of them. You've probably experienced this yourself; think of the last time that you saw a car change lanes without indicating, or a time you gave way at a junction only to find that the car you were giving way to was actually turning and you could have pulled away had they indicated. Was it an old banger or a BMW?

Similar experiments have shown that people in a higher salary bracket are more likely to cheat in a dice game and are less willing to give up their time or money to help others. In one study, a researcher presented participants with a jar of sweets and told them that although the sweets were for children in a nearby laboratory, they could take some if they wanted. The participants who had previously placed themselves in a high social class rank, took twice as many sweets as people who felt that they were of a lower social class.

But, correlation does not imply causation! Maybe it's the other way around. Rather than wealth making people selfish, maybe the meanness of selfish people has made them well off? To investigate this, you need to remember something that I mentioned in the previous chapter. The brain does not know the difference between fact and fiction.

By priming people to simply think about money, you can encourage them to behave in a less altruistic and more solitary manner. An often replicated set of experiments were put together by Kathleen Vohs, an associate professor of marketing at the University of Minnesota.[11] In order to prime people with thoughts of money, her team had people count banknotes or unscramble jumbled-up money-related sentences. Other times people were asked to undertake tasks in a room where Monopoly money was on a table, or simply a picture of money was on a screen saver. Afterwards, participants were put into various situations. Some participants witnessed someone 'accidentally' drop some pencils right in front of them. Those primed with thoughts of money picked up fewer pencils than those that weren't. In another situation, the researchers gave volunteers a difficult puzzle to solve and told them to ask for help at any time. Those who had previously been reminded of money waited nearly 70% longer to ask for help than those who hadn't.

In the same study, participants were asked by someone for their help with a word-solving problem. Those that had been previously primed with money images spent only half as much time assisting them compared to those that hadn't been.

It's as if thinking of money puts you in a frame of mind in which you don't want to have to depend on others, and you don't want others to have to depend on you. This could easily lead to isolation and loneliness – not necessarily a good recipe for being happy. But, some may say that this frame of mind could also make people more self-reliant and lead them to work harder to achieve their goals. So, maybe we just need to find the middle ground that allows us to be self-sufficient but not selfish. I'm certainly not saying that money can't make you happy. It absolutely can. Having more money to spend is likely to mean you have better health, are able to spend more time with your family and have a greater feeling of control over your life, which is a good recipe for happiness. But there is a threshold where it stops making much of a difference. After all, is someone earning £150,000 per year ten times happier than someone on £15,000? Not quite. If you look at the numbers collected by the Gallup organisation, it is true that there is a correlation between wealth and wellbeing. The greater the income, the higher that people place their wellbeing on a scale from 1 to 10. But if you were to plot the figures into a chart, you'd see that it's not a straight line; it's actually a curve. In fact the difference between £15,000 and £150,000 is actually just one single point. The 10-factor increase in income moves us from an average of 7 out of 10 to 8 out of 10 on the wellbeing scale. There is a specific point on the graph where it becomes incredibly difficult to derive extra happiness from your household income.

So, have a think for a moment. How much money do you think your household needs each year before any extra money stops making a significant difference to how happy you are?

Is it £100,000?

£150,000?

Nope, the absolute maximum a household can earn to have a positive effect on our happiness is about £50k per year.[12] That's two people earning £25k. Any more than that has been proven not to make a difference. Even households with a £1,000,000 income rarely make it up to 9 out of 10. In fact, a recent survey of US investors by global financial services firm UBS found that 70% of people with a spare million dollars in the bank and a six-figure income don't even think of themselves as wealthy. Only those that had $5 million or more in assets felt that they had enough savings to feel secure about their future.

We've known for quite a while that having lots of money isn't that important when it comes to being happy. In one famous experiment[13] in the 1970s, overseen by Philip Brickman, a group of lottery winners were compared with a random group from a phone book. The experiment revealed that the only difference between them was that the wealthier group found it far harder to derive pleasure from some of the simpler things in life, whereas enjoying a piece of music or even the smell of flowers was significantly easier for the average person.

This phenomenon even shows itself when comparing the wealth of various countries. Once a country gets to a moderate level of GDP, the happiness levels of its citizens begins to plateau and then eventually drop a little. Perhaps this explains why the happiest countries in the world I mentioned in the last chapter – Norway, Denmark, Iceland, Switzerland and Finland – are surprisingly low down the list in the rankings of national wealth. China is no happier now than it was 25 years ago, yet its GDP has increased fivefold in that period!

In April 2015, Nepal experienced its worst earthquake in recorded history. Known as the Gorkha earthquake, it killed nearly 9,000 people, injured almost 22,000 and left countless people homeless. Yet those that survived this tragedy became happier. Residents seemed more grateful for the things that they did have despite having lost so much.

Even though Nepal's main source of income – tourism – declined dramatically, the country moved up eight places in the World Happiness Index from 107 in 2016 up to 99 in 2017. Meanwhile, India moved down four places to 122 despite being one of the world's fastest-growing economies.

But, we're all different, aren't we? The things that influence one person might not influence another, and although you can look at studies that suggest having more money won't make you happier, it's easy to think of ourselves as the exception to the rule, isn't it? But we can't ALL be exceptions to the rule.

Take some time out to really think about this and maybe ask yourself a few questions. Here's one to start with:

Imagining that there is no change to the economy or the price of goods, which of these two scenarios would you prefer?

1. You and everyone else in the country gets a £10,000 pay rise.
2. You get a £15,000 pay rise but everyone else gets a £30,000 increase.

Think about it. Which one seems more appealing to you? Is it more money that appeals to you or more money than someone else?

Logically, scenario two should be more attractive as everyone benefits more than they do in the first scenario, including you.

But if the benefits of the extra £5k in the second one are being outweighed by some negativity that others are earning more than you, then it might be worth examining your motivations and priorities.

Here are another couple of scenarios for you to consider:

1. Your wages stay the same and your commute to work is 15 minutes.
2. You are offered a whopping 25% pay rise, but your commute to work is now one hour.

Which one would you prefer?

Are the extra 90 minutes per day travel time in scenario two worth the extra 25% wage increase? Or put it another way, are the extra 90 minutes per day free time in scenario one worth the lower salary?

Circumstances are different for everyone, but studies have shown that someone with a one hour commute to work has to earn 40% more than someone who has a short walk to work to obtain the same levels of life satisfaction.[14]

So, does more money make us any happier? The annoying answer is both yes and no. We need enough to cover our basic needs, but a higher salary doesn't necessarily mean greater wellbeing.

The relationship between money and happiness is a frustratingly complex one. Perhaps our focus should be less on how much we have, and more on how we spend it.

How To Spend It

In May 2009, Markus 'Notch' Persson, a Swedish computer software developer, released his own project to the public while continuing with his day job at a photo-sharing web company. His project – a block-based little adventure game which he would later call Minecraft – soon proved popular and within a very short time, Notch left his job and started up a company called Mojang so as to concentrate on it full time.

In early 2011, Minecraft sold its one millionth copy. By the summer of 2012 everybody under the age of 21 seemed to be playing it, and Notch had earned a whopping £60 million. The following year was even better still. But Notch wasn't happy. He had lost touch with his fans, because there were too many to interact with, and he was having more fun playing with prototype games than being involved with Minecraft.

As a prolific user of Twitter, in June 2014, he posted:

"Anyone want to buy my share of Mojang so I can move on with my life?"

Microsoft were listening, and in September 2014, Notch announced a deal to sell Mojang to them for £1.5 billion. Notch was a free man.

He outbid Beyoncé and Jay-Z for a £45 million Beverley Hills mansion with eight bedrooms, 15 bathrooms, a 16-car garage, an infinity pool, a wine cellar and even its own sweet shop. He could now do anything he liked. Notch's Twitter posts became a lot more positive after that!

But by August the following year, Notch's Twitter feed had started to look rather gloomy.

"The problem with getting everything is you run out of reasons to keep trying, and human interaction becomes impossible due to imbalance." (29th August 2015)

"Hanging out in Ibiza with a bunch of friends and partying with famous people, able to do whatever I want, and I've never felt more isolated." (29th August 2015)

Oh dear.

Notch, like many others before him, had fallen foul of what psychologists call 'hedonic habituation'.

A posh way of saying that the novelty wore off.

You may well have experienced this yourself at some point. The little thrill of a new phone or the excitement of a new car or even a new bread-maker. Within a short space of time, though, it feels no more exciting than the one you had before it. I'm afraid this is just what the brain does, and we need to put a little bit of effort in to prevent it. Being more grateful for the things you have in life might well be tricky, but it's not impossible. More of that later.

What happened to Notch and the countless lottery winners that have become rich beyond their wildest dreams is actually the same process as with the novelty of the bread-maker wearing off. Getting a new shiny thing may add value to your life at first, but it becomes less valuable to you each time you use it, until it holds no value to you at all.

Value is an interesting concept, though. There have been countless experiments that show us how our expectations will increase our pleasure in something. If we are told that something is valuable, then we will value it more and claim to enjoy it more. Give someone a glass of wine and tell them it's a top-of-the-range vintage, and they will rate it as much nicer than the one they were told is cheap plonk. Even if they're both the same wine. In fact, many professional wine critics have been duped into thinking that a cheap wine was expensive and an expensive one was cheap, and the experimenters stand back, smugly listening to them talking about how superior the cheap one was.[15] In his 1999 paper, published in *The International Journal of Vine and Wine*

Sciences, Frédéric Brochet, a PhD candidate at the University of Bordeaux II in Talence, France, explained that the critics he tricked would adjust their sensory perceptions to the quality suggested by the label. Context has a big part to play in how we value our experiences it seems, and being given information prior to experiencing something can lead us in different directions because of the placebo effect. We trick ourselves with our own expectations.

Brochet's experiments have even shown that you can dye white wine red and experts will still be duped.[16] Putting flavourless red food colouring into white wine, he tricked 54 wine experts into describing it as tasting of raspberry, cherry, cedar and chicory. The same wine when not dyed red was described by the same people as tasting floral, and of honey, peach and lemon. It turns out that wine-tasting really is a load of rubbish, after all.

Another astonishing example of the same phenomenon is with the Stradivarius violin. If you know nothing about violins at all, you might still be aware of the fact that a 300-year-old Stradivarius supposedly holds musical properties that modern violins can't possibly recreate. Some secret in the varnish or in the wood maybe. A secret that Antonio Stradivari kept hidden from the rest of the violin-making world, and hence why his violins can sell for up to £10 million. But guess what? In experiment after experiment, studies have shown that experienced classical music critics and even professional violinists cannot tell the difference between a violin made by Stradivari and a new one worth a fraction of its value.[17] In one of these experiments, ten renowned soloists each blind-tested six old Italian violins (including five by Stradivari) and six new violins during two

75-minute sessions, the first in a rehearsal room and the second in a 300-seat concert hall. When asked to choose a violin to replace their own for a hypothetical concert tour, they failed to distinguish new from old. Six out of the ten chose a new one believing that it was a Stradivarius.

So if we don't necessarily need the finer things in life in order to enjoy it, what should we do with our hard-earned cash?

In order to be happy, we need to spend our money on the right things. There are only so many 50" TVs and upgraded mobile phones we actually need, and because of hedonic habituation those new toys won't make us happy for very long and will soon become part of the furniture.

It turns out that spending money on experiences instead is a far better way of boosting our happiness.

Experiences are unaffected by hedonic habituation because we aren't being exposed to them over and over again. Instead we remember the emotion we felt at the time it happened.

One of the interesting findings to come out of this research is that there is a lot of pleasure in the build-up to experiences too. It can be great to have a last-minute weekend away, but deciding to do it a month in advance gives us something to look forward to, and knowing that there's something good coming influences our mood.

But all of this revolves around having a positive attitude; there's no point in planning your week away in advance just to spend six weeks worrying about whether the plane will crash. And if you're prone to negative thinking, then you're more likely to filter out the good stuff from your holiday and only really remember the restaurant with the bad service or getting sand in your hair one afternoon, rather than the restaurant with the really polite staff and the day at the beach, which despite getting sand everywhere, was an amazing day. So optimism and positivity are important skills to learn. And I call them skills because even if you inherit a high set point of happiness from your cheery grandma, you still need to make looking on the bright side second nature. Very little in life comes completely naturally to us. We blink, we breathe, we fall asleep and we digest our dinner. All of these things do come naturally to us – they're instincts. But anything that we repeat becomes natural to us too, and that's not because our personality was written in the stars – it matters not a jot whether you're a Sagittarius or a Virgo with the dark side of the moon rising. Personality is built over time through repetition of thoughts, feelings and behaviours, and so to create a whole new personality we have to create new thoughts, feelings and behaviours to repeat until they become second nature. It can be hard and might take a lot of practice, but with enough patience and enthusiasm for change, you can create a whole new personality irrespective of your horoscope. When we have a positive attitude, we tend to delete any bad experiences anyway; we'll flick through pictures of our holiday and continue to reinforce how good it was. But with a negative attitude, we can fall into the habit of wanting to complain all the time, leaving negative feedback everywhere we go on the off chance that we'll be compensated in some way.

Sure, putting in a complaint about your holiday might mean you get a voucher for a few hundred quid but deliberately tainting the memory of your holiday will decrease its long-term value no end.

But these experiences we buy to boost our happiness don't need to be as big as a holiday.

In one series of studies overseen by Dr. Elizabeth Dunn, associate professor in the Department of Psychology at the University of British Columbia in Vancouver,[18] 150 people were interviewed about their recent purchases. What the researchers found is that money spent on activities, like going out with friends for a meal and going to concerts, created far more satisfaction than material purchases did.

Interestingly, spending money on other people boosts our happiness more than spending it on ourselves. In the same study, 632 people were asked about their levels of life satisfaction and were also asked to disclose their average monthly expenditure broken down into categories. What Dr. Dunn found was that personal spending such as bills, living expenses and treats for themselves, made up an average of 90% of the outgoings but had no bearing on their happiness, whereas those that spent more money on other people by way of gifts or charitable donations, were much happier. This suggests either that altruistic spending will boost happiness, or that happier people are more likely to be selfless. In order to work out what causes what, Dunn and her team studied what happened to people if they received an unexpected bonus in their wage packet. They surveyed 16 employees at a Boston health industry company, measuring their levels of general happiness and wellbeing both before and after they were given a bonus ranging from $3,000 to $8,000. Two months later, when the researchers interviewed them again, they also asked about how they had spent the money. Regardless of the size of their bonus, the people who had spent the money in a selfless way ended up happier, while those who had spent it on themselves were no happier than before they had received the bonus.

In the third leg of their study, the researchers gave envelopes of either $5 or $20 to some students and told them to spend it all by 5pm that day. Some were told to spend it on themselves and others were told to spend the money on others by treating someone to lunch, buying something for a family member or simply donating it to charity.

When contacted later on that evening and asked some questions about how they were feeling, the people who had spent the cash on themselves described themselves as significantly less happy than the ones who had been told to spend it on someone else, regardless of how much money they'd been given to spend.

If experiences are better value for money than buying tangible items, then spend your time and money on something you will remember and gain pleasure from. Horseriding lessons are way cheaper than buying your own horse and come with a lot less sweeping up of poo.

Attending a pilates class is not only cheaper than those £100 Armani jeans but might also make your bum look better in the pair you already own.

Every now and again, go for a coffee, even if you're on your own and buy a random customer a drink. Buy a bottle of pop as you leave and give it to the first homeless person you see.

But if you're not convinced by this theory, try buying lots of cheaper things for yourself regularly instead of splashing out every once in a while. As Dr. Dunn discovered, because we adapt so readily to change, frequency is more important than intensity. So spending £10 on a treat for yourself once a week will have a greater effect than spending £100 every ten weeks.

Another interesting bit of research from 2017[19] showed that spending money on something that gives you time can have quite a significant effect too. In a study overseen again by Dr. Dunn, 60 participants were each given $40 and asked to spend it over the course of a weekend on things that would save them time. They bought things such as meal deliveries, paying neighbourhood children to help with errands or paying for cleaning services.

Then, on another weekend, they were all given $40 each again and told to spend the windfall on material goods. These ended up being things like clothes, wine and books.

After each weekend, the researchers contacted the participants and asked them how they were feeling. They were asked how much positive emotion they'd been experiencing as well as how much negative emotion. What it showed was that when participants spent money on time-saving services, they reported more positive emotion than they did when they spent the money on material goods. As well as buying yourself into positive experiences, this research suggests we should also consider buying our way out of the unpleasant ones. When surveyed, the research showed that even people with a super-high income and almost unlimited disposable cash still aren't outsourcing their disliked tasks much more than anyone does. And this effect is the same across the whole income spectrum; in a survey of over 6,000 people, ranging from millionaires down to the average Joe, those who spent money on something that gave them more time reported a greater satisfaction with life no matter which income bracket they were in. Even people in the lower bracket still had an almost 16% increase in life satisfaction compared to those that didn't outsource their tasks. This increase was almost one full point of wellbeing on the 1 to 10 scale, which if you remember could only be obtained through money if you multiplied your household income by a factor of ten by going from £15,000 to £150,000!

So, is there something you hate doing that fills you with dread just thinking about it? Cleaning the bathroom or mowing the lawn, perhaps? If so, then consider paying somebody else to do that for you, as research shows that's a pretty good use of your cash.

QUICK HAPPINESS BOOSTING IDEA

Take time to look through photos that you've taken over the last few months of the experiences you've had and keep those memories fresh.

MEASURING HAPPINESS

If you're going to be making some changes in order to get the most out of life, then it's very useful to monitor your happiness in the same way that the researchers I so often quote have done in their experiments. If you do this now, and then again in two weeks' time, hopefully you will begin to see some changes. This test should only take you a few minutes and there are no wrong answers or trick questions, so just go with the first answer that comes to mind.

Right then, take a look at the following statements and indicate how much you agree or disagree with each one according to this scale:

Can You Buy Happiness?

1 = strongly disagree
2 = moderately disagree
3 = slightly disagree
4 = slightly agree
5 = moderately agree
6 = strongly agree

You can write them on a separate sheet of paper if you wish, but do ensure that you write down the question number too.

1. I feel that life is very rewarding. _____
2. I often laugh. _____
3. I do not think that the world is a particularly good place. (R) _____
4. I have warm feelings towards almost everyone. _____
5. I do not feel optimistic about the future. (R) _____
6. I am able to deliberately find time for everything that I want to do. _____
7. When I think of my past, it is mostly the bad memories that I remember. (R) _____
8. I enjoy life, regardless of what is going on. _____
9. I don't tend to have much fun with other people. (R) _____
10. I get the most out of everything. _____
11. If I could live my life over again, I would not change very much. _____
12. I do not feel especially pleased with the way that I am. (R) _____
13. Compared to most of my peers I consider myself to be happier than them. _____
14. It is rare for me to wake up feeling rested. (R) _____

15. I feel that there is a gap between what I would like to do and what I have done. (R) _____

16. In general I consider myself to be quite a happy person. _____

17. I feel that my direction in life is controlled by other people. (R) _____

18. I find it relatively easy to make decisions. _____

19. If I attend a social function, I often feel I would rather be almost anywhere else. (R) _____

20. I have a good sense of meaning and purpose in my life. _____

Now that you have some figures, you need to do a little bit of work with them. Some of the questions need what's called reverse coding, which means you change a 6 into a 1, 5 into a 2, 4 into a 3, 3 into a 4, 2 into a 5 and 1 into a 6. Questions 3, 5, 7, 9, 12, 14, 15, 17 and 19 have an (R) next to them to indicate that they need reverse coding.

Done that? Good. Now tot up the score. It will be somewhere between 20 and 120. The higher the score, the happier you currently think of yourself. The average happy person scores about 80 with the more enthusiastic types around 90. Return to this questionnaire periodically and see what changes you can make.

Keeping Up With The Joneses

How much of your real life do you reveal to the external world around you?

If someone (other than a very close friend) were to ask you how you are, do you bombard them with your frustrations about your selfish spouse? Or about how you feel that your life is going by too quickly and there's a sense of impending doom everywhere you go?

Or do you say, "Fine thanks, you?"

On social media, do you post photos of yourself crying?

Do you write about loathing your boss, before starting a discussion with old school friends about the pointlessness of your existence?

For the vast majority of you, the answer to this is "Definitely not".

For some of you, those scenarios rarely come up anyway. But for a lot of you, they will. And a lot of your Facebook friends will go through those same emotions but will either not post anything at all about how they feel, or they'll simply lie about their life and post a photo or a quote or an article that completely disguises the truth about their situation. They might repost a photo of two people holding hands that says "Share if your partner is the best friend you'll ever have", while knowing full well that their partner is having an affair.

Why do so many people try to impress others in order to be proud of themselves? Is it to get one up on someone, as if thinking that we're better than someone in some way is the only way to be content in life?

I don't think anyone would ever give that advice to someone who was asking for the secret to happiness. Quite the opposite, in fact.

Once upon a time, it was only our relatives, close friends and colleagues that we compared ourselves with, but we can now see into the lives of billions of other people. Our relatives, close friends and colleagues are more than likely going to have a similar standard of living to you, but if on social media you mostly follow people living some millionaire lifestyle, then you aren't comparing like for like.

I'm sure we all know this but even so, looking at how great everyone else's life is seems to prevent us from noticing how amazing our own is.

And if so many people are creating this fictional version of themselves that doesn't exist outside of Facebook, then we shouldn't have anything to be envious about.

Yet so many people are, and keeping up with the Joneses can cause big problems. Even people that are high earners often live far beyond their means. If Mike Tyson and Meat Loaf can become bankrupt twice because they can't stop spending cash they don't have, what chance do we stand when our next-door neighbour gets a new kitchen on the same day that Barclaycard send us a pre-approved credit card that we didn't even ask for?

Buying things to impress others is often called 'conspicuous consumption' and is a term that was coined back in 1899 by the economist and sociologist Thorstein Veblen in his book *The Theory of the Leisure Class: An Economic Study in the Evolution of Institutions*. He used the term to describe the behaviours of the wealthy social class who came about as a result of the Second Industrial Revolution. Back then you either had money or you didn't, and that was that.

With credit cards and loans, things are a bit different nowadays, but people still flaunt their possessions to impress others. But just because our natural instincts say "Don't get left behind or you'll be someone's dinner", it doesn't mean we have to act upon those urges. Take a deep breath to remind your brain that you're safe, and evaluate your life. Do you actually need a £7,000 new kitchen? Or do you just need a new cooker and maybe some new cupboard doors? Don't let the misery of comparison deny you happiness and pride in what you already have.

The actual phrase 'Keeping up with the Joneses' comes from a newspaper cartoon strip in 1913, which ran until 1940. In the strip, the author poked fun at our need to do things to impress other people by depicting the social climbing McGinis family, who struggled to 'keep up' with their neighbours, the Jones family. And we still poke fun at these sorts of people, because we know that it's wrong and unnecessary. They're the characters in sitcoms that we laugh at. But despite this, there is this peculiar attitude among the majority that an ordinary life is a meaningless life – that just being OK is not enough. But it is!

The problem boils down to not being happy with whom you are and appreciative of what you have in the first place. We know that there's a correlation between materialism and self-esteem – loads of experiments have shown it – but it's one thing to know how the brain works; it's another to actually do anything about it.

So do yourself a favour. Stop wishing that you were someone else, or that you had what they have. Instead, start appreciating whom you are and the wealth that is already present in your life.

MATERIALISM EXERCISE

Check your spending habits over the course of the next month by making two lists. The first lists purchases of material things and the second lists the experiences you've spent money on. Add to it each time you spend money and after a month look through each list and consider the happiness that each purchase has brought you. Consider which items you are still as happy about now as you were when you bought them.

The African Violet Queen Of Milwaukee

Milton Erickson was an American psychiatrist who made famous the idea of treating the person and not the illness. While teaching in 1977, he told his students about an experience he'd had 20 years previously in which he had helped a man with severe confidence problems. A few months after his therapy had ended, the patient rang Dr. Erickson because he'd read that he would be teaching in Milwaukee. He asked Dr. Erickson if he could drop in and visit his ageing aunt; she was in a wheelchair and had become very withdrawn and depressed and had even dropped hints to her nephew that she was contemplating suicide.

Erickson agreed to his patient's request, so he finished his teaching workshop and went to visit this woman to hear her story. Now, Erickson had had polio as a child and walked with sticks, so when he rang the doorbell and this lady answered in her wheelchair, there was an instant bond between them. This was the 1950s and being 'handicapped' in those days often led to being ostracised. So it was quite a surprise for her to see how a man who struggled to walk could lead a successful life.

This lady had inherited a lot of money from her family and lived in a huge house with 12 rooms full of antiques, but she was alone. She had never married and never had children.

When she became ill, she fitted ramps and installed a lift

so that she could move around her home. And so, she was able to give Dr. Erickson a tour of her house.

All the blinds were closed. It was dark, gloomy and depressing. As she showed Dr. Erickson around, she told him about her life. Before she became ill she was a popular member of the community, was active in her church and had lots of purpose to her life.

But the last few years had been hard for her; the world wasn't wheelchair-accessible and even going to church was hard. She employed a man to take her to church, but it was still difficult getting in and out of the car. When she went to church, which was rarely, she deliberately arrived late and sat at the back where she wouldn't get in anyone's way. She would leave early so as not to inconvenience everyone because she needed to be lifted down the steps back to the car. She revealed to Dr. Erickson that this made her more and more withdrawn and depressed.

The last place the lady took Dr. Erickson to was her greenhouse. Dr. Erickson had grown up on a farm and so he took great interest in the plants she had been growing. As he looked along one shelf, he saw that there were pots and pots of little plants, and so he asked her about them.

The plants, the lady explained, were cuttings from her African violets. They're hard to grow and cultivate and she took great pride in growing them. Dr. Erickson was mightily impressed and he turned to her and said:

"Your nephew's very worried about you."

"I know he is," she said.

"He thinks you may be depressed," continued Dr. Erickson.

"Well, since the illness that put me in the wheelchair, I

have become withdrawn and unhappy, yes," she replied.

"But," said Dr. Erickson, "I don't think that's your problem."

"You don't?" she answered, brightening up a little.

"No," replied Dr. Erickson. "I think the problem is that you haven't been a very good Christian."

The lady came from a very moral and Christian background and was quite insulted.

"What do you mean?" she finally managed to ask.

"Well," said Erickson. "You have this great gift for growing African violets, you have all this time on your hands and all this money so that you don't need to work. And you keep it all to yourself. If I were you, I would get your church newsletter and membership list. And whenever someone had a birthday, or a death, a wedding, or an anniversary, or whatever, I would take them one of your beautiful African violet cuttings as a gift. Get your man to help you into the car and drive you to their house with your gift of the plant, your gift of condolences or congratulations and with your Christian human presence."

She listened to Erickson, admitted that she hadn't been the charitable Christian that she knew herself to be and told him that she would take his advice on board.

After that, Dr. Erickson left and never spoke to the lady again. But about ten years later, he received a letter from her nephew with a newspaper page. The headline read: "African Violet Queen of Milwaukee Dies... Mourned by Thousands." They couldn't fit all the people into the church that wanted to come to her memorial service because she had touched so many people in the last years of her life. She was always there to offer congratulations or condolences. Always there for others with nothing more than a plant and her Christian human presence.

When asked by students why he had given her that advice rather than prescribing medication, Dr. Erickson said:

"I looked all around her life, and everything looked depressing. She lived in this big house all alone. She kept the curtains drawn because she was embarrassed about being in a wheelchair. It was dark, it was lonely. The only sign of life that I could see in her and in her surroundings were those African violet plants. And I thought it would be easier to grow the African violet parts of her life than to weed out the depression."

And he was right.

She took what he said to her to heart. After he left, she began growing violets throughout her whole home. Windows were opened and light filled the previously dark house.

As her violets bloomed, she took them to people all over Milwaukee. She made friends and invited them over to see her violets. All of this led to her developing an incredible and fulfilling life of ministering to others.

So, whenever you start to experience down times, times in which you feel depressed or anxious, your focus can change. Instead of being able to focus on the positive, when we experience depression or anxiety, we tend to focus on our problems. And if we don't deal with them in a constructive manner, our outlook can become negative. Then we run the risk of becoming consumed or overwhelmed by our own negativity, or 'problem-focused' rather than 'solution-focused'. Focusing on the problems rather than the solutions will only make us feel worse.

Maybe one of the keys to guarding against having a negative

outlook is to deal with problems in the same manner that Dr. Erickson encouraged the African Violet Queen to do.

Don't try to weed out the negatives. Instead, grow the positive parts of your life.

Instead of focusing on your problems, focus on your strengths or on possible solutions to your problems. Try to remember what worked in the past. You are looking for exceptions to your problems or times when you didn't feel negative.

If you are feeling depressed, think back to a time when you weren't depressed.

What was different about that time? What were you doing differently that made you happy?

Find the exceptions to your problems. Become proactive in looking for things that cause personal satisfaction. If something made you happy before, no matter how small, start doing those things again.

Become solution-focused instead of problem-focused and grow your own version of the beautiful African violets.

QUICK HAPPINESS BOOSTING IDEA

Take 15 minutes out of your day every now and again to go through your food cupboard, see what you can find that you can take to the local foodbank donation point, and take it over there.

Self-Esteem And Materialism

Here's something I bet you didn't know.

The lower our opinion of ourselves is, the more likely it is that we will try and find pleasure in material goods. In other words, there is a correlation between materialism and self-esteem and it works both ways.

There's an experiment[20] that's been repeated quite a few times and keeps on showing the same results. Designed by Lan Nguyen Chaplin of the University of Illinois and Deborah Roedder John of the University of Minnesota, it was one of the first studies to focus on materialism among children. It revealed a strong connection between an increase in materialism during adolescence and a decline in self-esteem. Children between eight and 18 are tested, but it tends to work best with youngish children because they don't question why they're doing it too much and they make their decisions instinctively.

The children are asked to fill out questionnaires about how they feel about themselves, ticking boxes against statements like: "I am happy with the way I look." And, "I find it easy to take criticism."

Then they're shown some display boards with images on them, all relating to one of five topics (sports, people, hobbies, achievements and material things). Each child is then asked to make a collage of the images based around the topic of "What makes me happy?" It's then easy to work out a percentage of how many materialistic images the child chooses compared to the other four topics. Every time this study is undertaken, the experiment shows that there is a strong link between a low score on the self-esteem questionnaire and a high percentage on the materialistic test.

What you normally find is that there is a correlation with age as well; the older children tend to be more materialistic and score lower on the self-esteem test.

But could the cause and effect be the other way around? Remember, correlation does not imply causation! Just because there is a link, it doesn't always mean that they have anything to do with each other. After all, you could conduct a study in a high school that proves that having big feet makes you smarter by giving everyone the same test and comparing their results against their shoe size. The bigger the shoe size the higher the score will be. However, this would be a misleading result because the shoe size will be more of a reflection of their age than their intelligence. Similarly, maybe in the self-esteem vs materialism study, the materialism comes from something else, and whatever that something else is also lowers self-esteem. It would be bad science not to check this out. So Lan and Deborah got another group of children, only this time, before the children filled out the questionnaire, they were asked to spend some time writing nice things about other people in the group on a paper plate. And so, each child was presented with a stack of nice things about themselves, which had a huge influence on the self-esteem questionnaire that they filled in shortly afterwards. This also heavily influenced the choice of collage that they made. It was especially noticeable in the 16-18 year-olds, where the amount of material things in the collages had halved! This clearly shows that increased self-esteem leads to a decreased interest in material things.

So we shouldn't be treating ourselves and others with too many material things to try and influence happiness. It just won't work. Instead, we need to give each other a paper plate with "You are fun to be around" on it.

What all these different experiments show is that the psychological benefits of being given a gift don't lie in the gift itself but the fact that someone thought highly enough of you to give you something. Literally, it's the thought that counts.

When it comes to materialism, what we find is that the biggest influence we can have to boost happiness when buying something is to buy it for someone else. Treating someone else makes us feel happier than treating ourselves. Researchers at the University of Oregon used fMRI scans to see how the brain reacts when you play a game that involves either financial taxation or voluntary donation to people in need. The original purpose of their study was to figure out how the brain's pleasure circuit responded to differing approaches to giving and paying taxes, and it showed a fascinating insight into our brain's wiring.

At the start of the experiment, 19 people received $100 and were told that whatever they did with the money throughout the experiment was private (even the experimenters wouldn't know), but they would be able to keep whatever money remained at the end of it. They then lay in a brain scanner for an hour, while a computer screen showed them a series of possible money transfers to a local foodbank. In half of the transactions, they had a choice whether or not to make a donation. The other half of the transactions were compulsory, similar to a tax, and they had no choice in the matter. To further look at how the brain reacts, the screen would occasionally show money suddenly being taken away or added to either their own account or the foodbank's account.

What the experiment showed is that whenever we see money being given to a good cause, it produces a response in the same region of the brain that is responsible for pleasure, the ventral striatum. This is an ancient area of the brain that ensures we do things that keep ourselves alive so as to preserve the species. When the participants donated the money voluntarily it produced a much stronger activation of this pleasure response than the compulsory transactions did.

This is an instinct that has helped produce a happier and healthier species. And when it first developed we would have been so primitive we likely didn't even have the capacity for language, let alone finances. So, this pleasure response can be similarly activated by giving blood, volunteering, or even writing someone a thank you note.

When it comes to "It's the thought that counts" it works the opposite way around too; if you're doing something nice for someone else, not only will it boost their happiness but it will boost your own, probably through increasing your self-esteem slightly. One thing to bear in mind, though, would be some of the findings from happiness researcher Sonja Lyubomirsky of the University of California.

She and her colleagues looked into how non-financial acts of kindness influence our wellbeing, and what they found was that to have the most influence upon our happiness it's best to perform these acts of kindness one day per week. It doesn't have the same effect if it's too often. When participants in the study were asked to undertake five non-financial acts of kindness each week for six weeks, they found that the people who spread them throughout the week only showed a slight increase in happiness. By contrast, those people that did all five on the same day boosted their happiness by 40%. This is probably because if you repeat anything often enough it simply becomes habitual, and in some people that could even turn them into a bit of a doormat where they put other people first all the time. What you need to make habitual is feeling like a decent person rather than behaving like one. Doing something too often will make the behaviour so routine that it stops influencing the way that you feel. Once per week is fine, though, unless you're giving blood. Don't do that every week. That's a very bad idea!

Remember that when it comes to happiness at least, size doesn't matter. People often associate a huge price tag with huge happiness but it's simply not true. Rather than splashing out on a £700 new mobile phone every year, you could spend £35 twenty times and dine out with friends or family once per fortnight instead. These smaller costs that include social interactions like meeting someone for coffee or getting a spa treatment with a friend are a great way to create happy memories. Little bits of happiness soon mount up and will last a lot longer than the thrill of a new phone ever could.

QUICK HAPPINESS BOOSTING IDEA

Put your town name into JustGiving.com and see who is raising money for a good cause in your local area. Even if you don't donate anything to anyone, spending time looking at the good that's going on in your town will dilute down any doom and gloom you've picked up from elsewhere. But better still, chuck someone a fiver who won't be expecting it.

Journal Suggestions

1. Is there something in life that you can't imagine living without?

2. What do you love about life?

3. Imagine all goes well and you achieve your goals in life. What's your ideal future like?

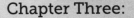

Chapter Three:

Adopt the Gratitude Attitude

What Is Gratitude?

So, we discovered in the previous chapter that the benefits of giving and receiving work both ways. But if it's you that's on the receiving end, then we also need to make sure that we're grateful for it, even if all we've received is a compliment.

Maybe it's a British thing, but so often I hear someone say something nice about someone else, and the recipient almost disagrees with it. One woman says to another "That blouse is nice" and the default reply is, "Oh, this old thing?" That's not fair, we should be grateful for the comment and say, "Thank you". There's nothing wrong with that; it's not big-headed to agree with someone if they say something nice about you.

In fact the concept of being grateful is probably the biggest ingredient to happiness, because it's one of the most effective methods for increasing long-term life satisfaction. Because of hedonic habituation, we can get very used to the good life and take a heck of a lot for granted.

There are people in this world who have almost nothing, but they are still thankful for what they do have and are happy.

I've heard many people's stories of trips to the slums of India that humble them to the point of making them question their lives.

I met a man recently who made some acquaintances in India through his work and when he retired he continued to go over once a year to see them. He wanted to treat one young man in particular who had as close to nothing as you can imagine, and so he took over an extra suitcase full of trainers and clothes for him.

When this young man saw these four pairs of trainers he said, "Why so many? I only have two feet," and then proceeded to wander around his village looking for people to give the extra three pairs away to, along with most of the clothes.

When my friend asked this young man if he wanted to use his hotel room to take a bath, it blew his mind! The idea of being able to have a bath in hot water was a huge thing to him, something he'd never ever been able to do. He actually asked if everyone in Britain had access to hot water, and when my friend told him that we do, he shook his head and said, "What? Even the poor ones?", and it made my friend question just what being poor really meant.

With each generation that goes by, we have become more and more privileged. Everyone seems to want to create a better life for their children and the next generation grows up not noticing how good their life is. In order to be happy, we need to take notice, but if gratitude isn't something that comes naturally to us, then we need to practise it until it does.

As I've already said, anything that you repeat enough times becomes a skill, something that you can do without effort, even gratitude.

But what do I mean by gratitude?

Gratitude is more than just a behaviour; it's more than just saying "Ta" when someone holds a door open for you.

As a process, gratitude is the acknowledgement of something good in your life. But it's also an emotion, a feeling of happiness that comes from appreciating whatever the source of that good something is.

When it's spread throughout the day, that feeling becomes a mood. And when you're in a grateful mood, you are more likely to find extra reasons to be grateful for other things, and so it grows ever stronger. When a mood is common throughout your life it becomes a personality trait that leads to a happier version of you.

For those of you with children that are either at school or have left, you'll be familiar with this situation.

"Hey mate, what happened at school today?"
"Nothing."
"Nothing, really? What lessons did you have?"
"Dunno, can't remember."

Now, when my son first started primary school, there was a novelty to it that meant that he couldn't wait to tell me all about it. But, within a few months the novelty had worn off and I didn't get to find out anything. I didn't want this habit to continue so I started playing a little game at night before he went to sleep. My wife and I would both come up with three things that happened that day that made us happy, or three things we were grateful for. Then it was his turn. For the first few nights, it was a struggle for him to play along because he couldn't really remember much. Which was why either my wife or I would do it first, to inspire him a little. So, I'd talk about something simple that would normally just go over my head, like how on my way back to my car that evening I saw a squirrel, and its little nose was twitching, it looked at me, grabbed a berry off the floor and then scampered up a tree, which made me smile. This would lead my son to say something like, "Harry farted in maths class and the teacher had to open a window."

But over the course of a few weeks it became a habit for him to look at things that were happening that made him happy and remember them, so that he could talk about them later. He began to filter his life only for the good things, and we can learn a lot from that process. If we're grateful for life then we can't be fearful, which means that any anxiety we experience gets processed as excitement instead. If we're grateful, then we act out of a sense that we have enough rather than out of a sense of scarcity or envy. This means we're more likely to give and share rather than take and hold. And we already know that giving and sharing pokes the happy buttons in our brain.

If we make something dominant in our mind, like gratitude, then we begin to filter our lives for reasons to be grateful and we begin to appreciate everything more.

There is an effect that in psychology is sometimes called the frequency illusion but is also known as the Baader-

Meinhof phenomenon. It's an effect that means we are more likely to be affected by things in our environment if we've been primed to think about them first. Which is why a woman who is thinking of starting a family is suddenly seeing pregnant women everywhere she goes. The frequency of pregnant women in her life hasn't changed. But she's filtering her world for the things that she thinks about.

This happened to me one year when my wife bought a new car, and suddenly I was seeing the same make and model of her car everywhere I went. They were always there beforehand but until one started appearing on my drive every day they weren't a part of my life, so I didn't notice them. I'm sure you've experienced the same phenomenon yourself, and because we're aware of it, we need to use it to our advantage, especially as research continually finds that being thankful can lead to a happier and less-stressed life.

But what do I mean by being thankful? I know that it can sound a little wishy-washy to proclaim that the secret to happiness is gratitude, as if we all need is to walk around wearing rose-tinted glasses and proclaiming that the flowers are lovely today like some 1960s hippy.

But there's a middle ground isn't there? A balance between being the hippy dancing around sniffing the flowers and being the grumpy sod who never appreciates anything, constantly acting like a victim. We don't need to go to extremes of gratitude in order to live a happy life; sure it can be an amazing life if we do, but it can seem unrealistic. If there's one thing known about goal setting that's constantly agreed upon it's that having an unrealistic goal will prevent you from getting started.

So instead of aiming to find huge joy in everything that

you experience, start by beginning to reject ingratitude first and see where it leads you.

AFFECTIONATE WRITING EXERCISE

There's been loads of research into the positive effects that 'affectionate writing' has on our life. It's even been shown to affect our physical health[21] as well as our mental health,[22] lowering cholesterol and reducing stress.

Spend 15 minutes writing about some positive things that have happened to you. Write about some of the good things that you'd like to see happen in the future. Write about things that you plan to do. Write with passion and enthusiasm.

Write with affection about the people that are important to you, how you feel about them and your hopes for them. Write one of these people a letter telling them about how important they are to you. You don't have to actually give it to them, although if you did it would certainly have a very positive effect on both of you.

On the days when you don't get the opportunity to write about these things, make sure you at least go to bed with a small list on your mind of the reasons to be grateful. Three things that happened that day that were positive. Or three things you've experienced in your life that you're grateful exist.

Perspective

If you were to stop someone in a supermarket and ask them if they are ungrateful, most will probably reply, "Of course not!" or "How dare you!" or "Help! Security!" However, being ungrateful has become so ingrained into society, that people do not even realise that it forms such a part of their personality.

So, how do you tell if you are ungrateful? Are there behaviours or thoughts that identify it? And if so, what can you do about it?

Merriam-Webster's Dictionary defines ingratitude as 'Forgetfulness of, or poor return for, kindness received'. But if there's a sliding scale of ingratitude, then I think it can also be defined as simply not appreciating what you have. So ask yourself this question every now and again throughout your day: "Did I take that for granted?" It could be the fact that you made a cup of tea without having to start a fire by rubbing two sticks together for an hour first. By not taking it for granted, you might find that you enjoy that cup of tea a little more. After all, how much would you enjoy it if you did have to rub two sticks together for an hour to start a fire first? It would probably be the best cup of tea you'd ever had...

The next time you fly anywhere, take a moment to think about the alternative. Are you going to drive to Cyprus instead? Good luck! But it's too easy to complain that the seat on the plane isn't that comfy, that the food is a bit rubbish, that you had to wait for the plane to take off for five minutes longer than you'd expected. There's always a better perspective. The plane might not be the comfiest of environments, but you're flying through the sky for goodness sake! Look out of the window for a moment and say "Wow!"

I was involved in a minor car accident a few years ago. Fortunately, nobody was hurt. In fact, the driver of the lorry that crunched into the side of me didn't even drop his ice cream, which goes to explain just how the accident occurred.

I'd only had the car a few months and I was a tad annoyed to say the least to see the passenger door caved in and the front bumper hanging off. However, there wasn't anything I could do about it. A part of me wished I'd left the house five minutes earlier – that way I wouldn't have been involved. But, I realised that all that would have happened was that someone else would have been on the receiving end of the ice cream-eating lorry driver who wasn't looking where he was going, and they might not be as resilient as me. If there was a choice between me and a 77-year-old pensioner driving an old Mini Cooper being bashed into by ice cream guy, I'd rather it was me. After all, it's too easy to say, "Why me?" when something bad happens, but what's so special about me that I should be immune to getting hurt? Why not me? Would I deliberately choose to put someone more vulnerable in harm's way? Of course not. I'd much rather it was me that needed to clear my thoughts, take a few deep breaths and carry on with my day than a 17-year-old who had only just passed their test and was so frightened that they vowed to never drive again. And I know those sorts of things happen because I see those people as clients later on in their lives.

Even in difficult situations that cause great upset, there's still a better perspective. It's likely that at some point in your life you have met someone diagnosed with terminal cancer that is still enjoying life, and then shortly afterwards met someone who has an ingrowing toenail that can't stop complaining about it.

A few years ago, when my son was at primary school, my wife and I went to collect him one day and had to park quite a distance away from the school gates. Anyone with children knows the frustration of 400 under-12s all needing collecting at the same time. Every day feels like the last shopping day before Christmas, and every now and again my son would come home with a letter from the school asking all parents to park their cars respectfully of the home owners in the area. It was not an uncommon sight to see someone walk out of their house to go somewhere and be unable to get off their drive because a BMW or an Audi (almost never an old banger, see page 60) had blocked them in. So, this particular day we're walking the 300 yards or so down the road and my wife spots that a car has parked in such a way that, had it parked slightly further forwards, then another car would have been able to park behind it without blocking anyone's driveway. "You see," she said, "that gets on my nerves." I asked her how much it bothered her, on a scale of 1 to 10. And after she shook her head a few times and asked why I always turn everything into a psychology game, she reluctantly said that it was probably about 7 on the angry scale. So, I pointed out the dozen or so cars that were all parked in such a way that made it easy for home owners to get off their drives and also were making maximum use of space. I asked her on a scale of 1 to 10 how happy it made her to see that things were being done the way she liked it. After a bit more head shaking and comments questioning why she married me, she claimed it was zero. Seeing things done the way she likes it has no influence on her happiness but things done the way she doesn't like it influences it massively. My attitude tends to be that we shouldn't allow ourselves to be influenced by the negatives if we don't also allow ourselves to be influenced by the positives. And that's why it's important to ask yourself the question: "Am I taking this for granted?" from time to time.

To show the effects of *wanting what you have* compared to *having what you want,* a research[23] study was undertaken at Wichita State University where participants had to look through a list of 52 material items and indicate which ones they already owned. Then they were asked to rate how much they wanted each item, even the ones they already had. They were also asked to take part in questionnaires about their life satisfaction and overall wellbeing. It showed that participants who said they wanted the things they already had were far happier than the individuals who had grown accustomed to their material possessions. It also showed that our desire for the things we don't have needs to be monitored, as those who perceived themselves as being satisfied with nothing less than the best were noticeably unhappier.

Think of it like this. Do you remember the last time you had a heavy cold? It was only a minor irritation in the grand scheme of things, but it was one you could have done without, I'll bet. The streaming eyes, the crummy feeling in your stomach, the sneezing out of mucus equal in weight to your entire head. I bet you'd have loved to have been able to breathe easily, wouldn't you? And then finally, there was the relief of it clearing up. You woke up one day and realised that you could breathe through your nose again – how wonderful!

How long was it before you took it for granted that your nose was working properly again, I wonder? An hour? A day? Because of habituation, we get used to things quite quickly and we normalise everything. That's why someone with a house full of dogs doesn't notice how bad it smells. It's just what the brain does to keep it efficient – it deletes all the things in your experiences that are no longer a surprise to you. It fades them into the background so as to better organise everything else going on in the circuitry of our brain. So, we have to work a little harder at bringing the things we take for granted in life out of the background and into our conscious awareness.

When things blend into the background of our awareness and become unconscious, they don't jump out at us any more. Things like running water, electricity, the emergency Cup a Soup in the kitchen cupboard, our health, our friends, access to the internet.

These things have all become such a constant that they become part of the wallpaper of our life. To stop taking them for granted, we need to bring these things out of the unconscious background and into our conscious awareness, but it takes deliberate action to do that. I know it sounds like hard work, but as I've constantly emphasised to you, anything that you repeat enough times becomes second nature, habit and a part of your personality.

So, make yourself consciously aware of what you're doing and what's around you throughout your day.

Be consciously aware that you can easily get clean water with just the turn of a tap. Consider all the planning and designing it must have taken to get it to you.

Be consciously aware that you can easily find the answer to almost any question you have with just a quick search of the web. Consider that someone had to write the article that gave you the answer, they took the time to do that for your benefit and they spent money making that website for you to read.

The same goes for everything. The next time you make a cup of tea, look at all the steps it took just so you could slurp a mouthful of leaf-steeped warm water. The tea bag alone is complicated enough, let alone designing your kettle and your mug, as well as the delivery of electricity to your home and into your kitchen.

The next time you're hungry and you eat something and feel satisfied, just think about how complicated your body is. From a humble cheese and tomato sandwich, your body is able to use the constituent carbohydrates both simple and complex, vitamins, minerals, proteins and fibre. Energy that powers everything from your heart pumping blood to the ability to laugh at someone tripping over their cat.

Once you make yourself aware of how big even the small things in life actually are, you can begin to appreciate them more. If you're struggling to do that, imagine what life would be like without the things you take for granted. Think about how you'd make a cup of tea if everything man-made suddenly disappeared and you had to do it all yourself.

The fact that this sort of attitude can have beneficial side effects perhaps means you're more likely to look after your health and are more inclined to make sure your car is serviced regularly. After all, both of those things will come back and bite you on the bum if you don't. It's only after your car breaks down that you'll realise how important it was to you, and it's then that you'll wish you'd looked after it better. The same goes for your body. It's only after you fall off your son's skateboard and pull a muscle in your back that you realise you should have taken up tai chi or pilates when it was first recommended to you by your osteopath. I speak from experience here.

We shouldn't have to have something taken away from us before we recognise how important it is to us, should we?

How many times have you heard the phrase, "You don't know what you've got till it's gone"?

Think about 'John' for a moment.

John takes his car for granted. He really loved it when he first got it, he treated it respectfully, listened to how it sounded and made sure he put effort in to ensure that any problems with it were sorted before they got any worse. Eventually though, he began to take it for granted. He treated it with a little less respect with every month that went by and he doesn't even notice that it's no longer acting the way that it used to. As a result of this neglect, the car has broken down on him and it looks like it's beyond repair.

Now think about John's scenario again... only this time, instead of it being his car, it's his girlfriend, and it's his relationship that is beyond repair. Or imagine it's his health and it's his body that stops functioning properly.

In any of those situations, if John had been more conscious of what he was experiencing, if he had pulled things out of the background of his awareness and into the foreground, then he would have been able to consider life without it. He would have been more compelled to look after the things in his life that are important and prevent them from being lost to him.

I can't emphasise enough the positive emotional impact that not taking things for granted in your life will create. It allows you to live a life with a sense of plenty rather than one of scarcity, which prevents jealousy and envy. It's the difference between having everything you want and wanting everything that you have.

You can still want more from life; wanting what you have doesn't mean that life is perfect and doesn't need improving, it means that you have chosen to accept and appreciate what you do have first, in order to feel good enough to take the steps that let you seek out more.

QUICK HAPPINESS BOOSTING IDEA

Take a moment or two to send a text message to someone thanking them for being a part of your life. It doesn't have to be particularly fancy, simply thanking them for making you smile that day is enough. See these ideas as confirmation of how fortunate you are, despite any negatives that may have gone on in your life. It will remind you that good things can and do happen to you.

Jenny

About ten years ago I met Jenny, a young woman with cystic fibrosis. She was 20 at the time and felt enormously grateful that she had got that far. When she was born, her condition was so bad that her parents were told that she'd be lucky to see her teenage years. There is no cure for CF.

If you don't know what it is, CF is a genetic disease that clogs up the lungs and digestive system with a thick sticky mucus that makes it hard to breathe, exercise and digest food. It is unforgiving and relentless and will result in an early death usually because the bacteria in mucus reproduces and causes pneumonia.

But rather than wrap her up in cotton wool and treat her like a precious glass ornament, her parents encouraged her to live her life as her peers did, with the exception of needing to spend 40 minutes clearing her lungs of the thick, sticky mucus every morning, noon and night.

Yes, she was different in that bits of her body didn't work properly. But she could still do the same things as everyone else; she just had to do them differently.

She learned how to climb trees, how to ride a bike, and she grew up happy in the knowledge that life is for living. She always knew she would die young, but even from an early age she would talk about it casually as if it was nothing more than moving house. She was only four years old when she turned to her parents one day while playing on a beach and said, "When I die, bring me here," and she ran off to splash in the sea, leaving her speechless parents trembling on the sand.

Even at 11 years old, just to eat a normal meal she needed to take more than 20 tablets for her body to process the food properly. Her school friends couldn't believe it. "Take them all in one go!" they would say, and she would. But only if they gave her ten pence. She gave all the money to a charity that looked after retired greyhounds.

When she was 15, she learned to repair cars and became enthusiastic about mechanical engineering. If she wasn't welding something, she had her head in a car engine. She was happy.

She'd already had a liver transplant and next on the list would be a lung transplant, but she refused it. "If a car is broken," she said, "you don't bother putting new parts into it." She felt that a new pair of lungs would be wasted on her, that the extra couple of years it might add to her life were not worth the hassle. She wasn't looking for more time, but instead she just wanted to enjoy the time that she had. As far as she was concerned, another operation and stronger anti-rejection medication wouldn't improve her life.

It was recommended by all of her doctors that she see a counsellor to help her come to terms with the reality of her mortality. She followed their advice, but it seemed pointless to her. She had already come to terms with her mortality, but her counsellor was convinced her happiness and enthusiasm for life must have been some sort of defence mechanism, as if she didn't fully understand that she was dying. She was told she needed to take it more seriously and that she should expect to be depressed. Jenny refused to believe that in order to understand mortality she needed to be negative about life, and so she became less and less interested in the therapy sessions. Eventually her counsellor suggested that they stop therapy as she was obviously not gaining any benefit. It was suggested that if she wanted to monitor her mental health she should try something different, which led her to me.

I specialise in hypnotherapy and so the sessions were a little different to her than her counselling sessions had been. The novelty of doing something new and different kept her engaged, and maybe she opened up more to me than she did with her previous therapist. She had a huge passion for life and wanted to see and experience as many new things as she could, revelling in the idea of simply doing, as she put it, "something else, whilst I've still got the chance".

So we worked on her confidence, using techniques to make her feel even more independent, like helping her to jump into her car and disappear to the other end of the country for a weekend if she wanted to.

One technique we used is often referred to as parts therapy. It's the concept that our personality is made up of many different components. There's a part of us that wants to laugh, but also a part that wants to cry. A part that feels scared, but a part that shows bravado. These 'parts' to our personality are very normal but sometimes are in conflict with each other, causing anxiety. It's often the reason why smokers will continue to smoke, gamblers will gamble and alcoholics will drink. The part that wants to continue with the damaging behaviour is more dominant than the part that wants to quit it. Finding a common interest that these parts share is useful in order to accept them and move on.

Often all parts of us have the same core goal, simply to try and make us happy. The parts to Jenny's personality were all trying to do just that, make her happy. Acting as if she didn't have CF made her happy, acting as if she wasn't scared of dying made her happy. But acknowledging her illness would make her happy too; it gave her more drive than most people have, in order to see things and experience her world more fully and more appreciatively.

As her confidence grew, she decided to do some travelling. She bought some camping supplies and would spend days on end in the middle of a wood hundreds of miles from home. One morning at 2am, her parents received a phone call for no reason other than to tell them that she'd seen a stag outside her tent. She knew she had CF and that there was no escaping it, but she'd be damned if it was going to stop her enjoying herself.

A few years before she died, Jenny needed a percutaneous endoscopic gastrostomy (PEG) feeding tube to keep up with her body's need for nutrition. Without it, each meal would have to be more than twice the size of everyone else's just to get the same calories, and this meant that meals were becoming a chore and were not enjoyable any more. A PEG tube is inserted directly into the stomach and connected to a food pump or syringes that keep you topped up with calories and nutrients while you rest. Using one means that you don't need to consume quite as much during normal meal times, making them more enjoyable. However, the PEG tube is uncomfortable and difficult to hide under clothing, especially as needing one often means you're underweight anyway.

Jenny didn't want people to know how ill she was, so she hid the tube as best she could. She started wearing baggier clothes to hide it and stopped wearing dresses. It made a part of her happy keeping it a secret, but it made another part of her sad. She began to feel less feminine, her confidence dropped again, she started to feel unhappy with her body and her self-esteem began to fall. So she asked her Mum for a favour.

"Would you take some photos of me?" she asked, to which there's only one sensible answer.

"Of course," her mum replied.

But then Jenny added, "Naked photos."

"Errrr?"

"Whilst running through a bluebell wood."

"Ermmm? I guess so!"

So they did. They found a place and made sure no one was around, Jenny took off her clothes, showed her feeding tube to the world and posed for picture after picture. They were all tasteful, artistic and quite beautiful. She had some printed and hung on the wall in her hallway for her to see every day to remind herself that she was a woman, and every day her confidence improved. Every time she walked past those pictures, her self-esteem rose a little. She started wearing more feminine clothes again and began to accept the feeding tube for what it was, a way of being able to relax and enjoy going out for a meal with friends and family again.

Jenny would ring me every six months or so to fill me in on the upgrades to the 4x4 that she was working on and ideas of how to do up campervans and motorhomes. She worked part time and despite her energy levels being very low, she enjoyed her job and refused to give up work. She hid the fact that she had cystic fibrosis so well that many people at her funeral didn't even realise that she had it.

She died as happy as anybody possibly could, laughing so hard at her mum getting a bedpan tangled in the medical equipment cabling that she literally almost died laughing the night before she actually did pass away.

One of the things I was told when completing training was that there is a limit to how much you can learn in a classroom, that our clients will be the ones that teach us more than a classroom ever could. And it's true.

Jenny taught me that true happiness means we're able to accept that bad things can happen to us but that they should never overshadow the good. She didn't take her life for granted because she knew that it could be so easily taken away, and because of this she took advantage of any opportunity she could find that could lead to pride or pleasure.

She was genuinely embracing life because of her illness, not just despite it. And when I realised that this wasn't just a defence mechanism, it made me question my own levels of contentment. Sure, I was happy. I was in a wonderful relationship, my wife and I had recently started a family and

I was very happy in my career. If I was to make a list of all the things to be grateful about, surely my list would be longer than hers and therefore surely I should be happier than she is.

And yet here she was, this young woman talking about her impending demise in the same way that I might talk about the weather. She still felt angry that she was going to die young and she still had a fear of the future from time to time. But it wasn't damaging her happiness levels, because she went out of her way to enjoy what was going on in her life at that moment. She even said that she felt kind of grateful at times for her illness, that if it wasn't for CF she wouldn't be able to have the experiences that she was having. She'd have to work full-time and, like everyone else, would probably never get around to experiencing them.

It made me realise that if she can be this grateful for life, then I should be the happiest man on earth.

QUICK HAPPINESS BOOSTING IDEA

Leave a sticky note for someone, telling them how great they are. Stick it to their computer screen when they leave their desk or hide it inside a book they're reading.

Maybe leave one somewhere for a total stranger to see, with a message on it to lift their mood.

It's a bit wacky, but if you have a sense of humour as strange as mine you could even write a comedy shopping list of ridiculous items and leave it in a supermarket basket. Writer Robert Popper is perfect at this, supplying such gems as 'angry paint', 'Mars bar spray' and 'horse deodorant (roll on)'.

Cecilia

One of the reasons why I became a therapist was because of the experiences I had when I was 16 and accidentally found myself volunteering at my local hospital. As a teenager, I was interested in a career in broadcasting and one of the easiest ways to gain experience in that sort of thing was to work with a hospital radio station.

If you don't know what hospital radio is, imagine a student radio station that only plays music if it's more than 30 years old. It's a bit like that.

Now the first thing to happen to new members at a hospital radio station is that you get put on the wards, for a couple of different reasons. Firstly, you need to get to know your audience and find out what sort of music they'd like to listen to while they're in hospital (almost always Jim Reeves, it seems). And secondly, to work out which of the new members was prepared to actually do any work other than just pretend to be a DJ. And it was because of these experiences that I became intrigued by human nature. It got me interested in psychology and showed me about alternative ways of thinking and feeling about problems. Not just because one patient may have a different pain threshold to another, although that did fascinate me and fuelled my interest in hypnosis, but because some patients had a foundation to their personality that allowed them to see past their physical ailments and be positive and happy.

When I first met Cecilia, she had recently come into the hospital aged 73 suffering from a condition called Raynaud's syndrome. Raynaud's is a circulatory problem that affects the blood supply to certain parts of the body. Blood vessels go into spasm and block the flow of blood to the extremities. This caused her little finger to become oxygen-deprived and begin to die, so it needed to be amputated. She was super-cheery about it and made many jokes about burying it in a matchbox and giving it a funeral. Unsurprisingly, she asked me to play her some Jim Reeves and laughed when I asked her if there was a particular track of his that she'd prefer. She looked down at her blackened finger and said, 'He'll Have To Go'.

I saw her again a week later and she thanked me for playing it. She showed me her bandaged hand and told me that although there was a slight infection she was on the road to recovery and would probably go home the following day. This time she asked me to play her 'You Need Hands' by Max Bygraves.

The next week, I was surprised to see her still on the ward, and I sat with her to see how she was coping. "Any day above ground is a good day," she said. The infection hadn't quite healed though, probably due to the Raynaud's preventing blood flow, and so she was being kept in for maybe another week. She said that she felt fine about it and made jokes about bad hospital food still being better than the rubbish her husband could put together. She asked for 'Release Me' by Engelbert Humperdinck this time.

Well, they did release her and so I didn't see her for around six months. But she was brought back into the hospital because she needed another finger amputating. It was looking as if the Raynaud's was a symptom of something more serious.

From that point up until she died, two years later, Cecilia never left the hospital. I saw her most weeks, and every single time I saw her she was laughing about something. Yet, almost every time I saw her there was a little more missing from her body. Every month, another finger or two needed to be removed, then some toes.

Soon her feet, then her hands were amputated. Eventually her arms and her legs needed removing. But she continued to be happy. She spent time thinking of more songs that would be amusing to request, including 'The First Cut is 'the Deepest', 'Footloose' and 'Wide Eyed and Legless'. I was convinced that she must have a copy of *The Guinness Book of British Hit Singles* tucked away somewhere.

If someone asked her how she was feeling she'd say "Any day above ground is a good day, how are you?"

She was genuinely interested in other people and loved hearing about what we'd all been doing outside of the hospital. She had no envy in the slightest, despite the fact she was unable to leave her bed, and took great delight in catching up on the gossip from the hospital social club.

Looking at her life from the outside you'd think it would be a miserable one, but she embraced everything she could with positivity and joy.

We spent a lot of time together towards the end of her life, and I was able to learn a lot from her. She told me that she knew what the prognosis was very early on in her diagnosis. She knew she was going to lose her body little by little until it simply stopped working and she would die, but she refused to feel like a victim. She told me that she'd had a wonderful life and had no reason to be angry that it would be cut short so quickly. Knowing that at some point soon she would lose all of her limbs meant that she appreciated them more while they were still working.

The last time I saw her was when I was giving out bingo

cards to patients who wanted to play along with me later on in the day. Cecilia had wasted away; her body wasn't absorbing nutrients from her food and she was almost unrecognisable. She was nothing more than a torso and a head. But, she was still able to be happy. We would laugh and joke together and she embraced what was left of her life, even joining in with the bingo game with everyone else, just with a marker pen in her mouth.

Mindfulness

One of the most useful studies in recent times into happiness was put together by a man called Matt Killingsworth.[24] As part of his doctoral research, he came up with the idea of using smartphones to monitor what people were doing and how they felt doing it. Putting data from thousands of users into a computer, he was able to use it to figure out what makes us happy and what makes us miserable.

It turns out that people enjoy having sex more than they do being at work, which came as no surprise. But what did come as a surprise was that when people were resting, literally doing nothing, they were no happier than they were at work and no happier than they were when simply watching TV. Being at work and resting were among the lowest on the list of things that make people happy. This was interesting to me because one of the things people often look forward to if they are at work and unhappy is their time off, where they can go on holiday and chill out. Yet doing nothing makes us no happier than if we'd just stayed at work.

According to Killingsworth, this peculiarity is more than likely down to mind wandering, because relaxing and doing nothing gives us too many opportunities to worry about things. Sure, go on holiday and chill out. After all, we need some downtime. Life isn't a race, and if it is then we don't want to be rushing to the finish line; we want to drag it out as long as we can! So if you do spend your cash on a holiday, make sure you don't spoil it by mind-wandering. Instead, enjoy the experience by focusing on the here and now. One way to learn how to enjoy the present moment is with what's called mindfulness meditation.

Our brain has the ability to make a lot of information it processes unconscious. Many experiences soon become outside of conscious awareness and thoughts and behaviours soon take less effort. Sounds great. That's how skills are developed and that's how we learn to play complicated musical instruments. What could possibly go wrong?

Unfortunately this doesn't just apply to how well we can walk, talk or play the didgeridoo. It also means that we can eat a bag of peanut M&M's with hardly any recollection of eating them and so still feel unsatisfied. It means that we can buy some expensive shower gel in a shop and think that it's wonderful, but the next day when we take a shower on autopilot we're hardly even aware of how nice it is because in our minds we're already at work dealing with a pile of paperwork.

Mindfulness is a very simplified form of meditation that helps to improve our ability to bring things into the present, and has some very beneficial effects upon the brain and body. Research has shown that adding mindfulness into your life has a very positive effect upon the regions of the brain that are related to attention and sensory processing[25] with the potential to even offset the effects brought on by the ageing process and Alzheimer's disease. Dr. Sara Lazar, of the Massachusetts General Hospital Psychiatric Neuroimaging Research Program, was one of the first to study how mindfulness meditation affects the brain. Dr. Lazar and her colleagues took scans of the brain structure of 16 participants before and after they took part in an eight-week Mindfulness-Based Stress Reduction programme. Mindfulness has long been shown to have a positive effect upon wellbeing, but it was often argued that maybe people were feeling better simply because they were spending more time relaxing. What this, and further studies show, is that mindfulness strengthens our brain in three key areas.[26]

Firstly, there's the prefrontal cortex. This is the newest part of our brain to have evolved and is pretty much responsible for everything that you might think about. It has given us the ability to perceive what might happen in the future, so that instead of throwing a spear at where the chicken is now, you throw it at where it is going to be in a few seconds' time, when the spear lands. Without it, we'd still be living in caves occasionally running out for a berry or two, so it has become very useful to us. It plays a significant part in problem solving, emotion regulation, pursuing goals and inhibiting counterproductive impulses.

Secondly, there's the hippocampus. This is the part of the brain that has a critical role in learning and memory. Because of this, it is extraordinarily susceptible to stress, depression and Post-Traumatic Stress Disorder (PTSD). All of these things actually make it shrink, as if to hide us from our memories. An improved hippocampus helps us to deal with anxiety and depression as well as to help us remember what we went into a room for.

The third is the amygdala. MRI scans show that after just eight weeks of mindfulness practice, the amygdala begins to shrink. This ancient region of the brain is associated with fear and emotion, and is involved in the initiation of the body's response to stress. So, as the ability to be anxious gets slower and the ability to think clearer gets quicker, it becomes easier and easier to maintain a positive outlook to life.

So what is mindfulness and how do you practise it? Well, its origins go back thousands of years and are rooted in Buddhism. It was advocated as a path to spiritual enlightenment and a cessation of suffering, achieved through periods of meditation. This is done by sitting quietly, moving the focus of your attention away from the outside world, away from the past, away from the future and into the present moment. It involves separating thoughts from awareness, such as being aware of the cushion you're sitting on but not thinking about it, or being aware of the weight of your clothes on your body, but not thinking about them. Put simply, mindfulness is about learning to relax and be at peace with your thoughts. It can take a little time to become good at it, but it is well worth putting the effort in. People often make the mistake of thinking that they can't do it because their mind always wanders whenever they try to relax, but that's the whole point of mindfulness. It's about being aware that your mind wanders and learning how to better react to it. Someone with ten years' practice can maybe sit for 15 minutes and meditate without their mind wandering at all, but at first you might only be able to manage five seconds. That's fine. In 15 minutes of mindful meditation, you might only be doing it properly for five seconds at a time every five minutes, and the rest of the time your mind is busy thinking about all the jobs you could have done if you weren't trying to do this crappy meditating thing. That's fine. Keep at it and it soon becomes ten seconds every five minutes, then 20 seconds every four minutes. Maybe it will take months of daily practice before you can do it for a minute at a time and with only 30 seconds of mind wandering in between. That's fine. Your brain is getting more efficient every day that goes by, dealing with stressful situations gets easier and easier, making decisions becomes effortless and your faith in yourself becomes stronger and stronger.

Within a few months, you'll find that even when you're not meditating, the mindful attitude will be with you everywhere you go. It means that gratitude will become second nature to you. It will become easier to appreciate everything. You'll become happier. Those that really take to it and meditate for a whole hour every day show a significant increase in their happiness levels in just eight weeks.[27] In a 2003 study, overseen by Dr. Richard J. Davidson of the University of Wisconsin, researchers saw that there were demonstrable and measurable positive effects to mindfulness. This manifested as a positive increase, not just in their subjective "This is how I'm feeling today" reporting, but also an increase in the area of the brain responsible for making the emotions in the first place, the left side of the prefrontal cortex. Another finding revealed significant increases in antibodies in the blood in response to an influenza vaccine.

Now, an hour each day is a bit extreme and probably not necessary for most people, so 15 minutes is fine for now. But if you want to slowly move up to 30 minutes at some point in your future, it would definitely benefit you even more.

MINDFULNESS EXERCISE

To do this it's probably going to be helpful at first to find somewhere where you know you're not going to be disturbed. Somewhere with very few distractions, a spare room, a conservatory, or go and sit in your car in the garage if you fancy. When you meditate, it's important to acknowledge your thoughts rather than try to stop them. Earlier on in the book, I talked about thought stopping, about how to take your mind away from topics that could upset you and give you more control over how you use your mind, but that's not necessary when meditating. Thought stopping is for when you're being obsessive about a thought and is for other times and places. When meditating, you can allow thoughts to come and allow them to go again. What you'll find is that because of learning about mindfulness, you may not need to use the thought stopping exercise so much as your intrusive thoughts become quieter and quieter anyway.

There are lots of free resources around the internet for you to access that will guide you through how to do this. If you search for mindfulness meditation on YouTube, you will find thousands of exercises to listen to, but once you've got the idea you may well find you can do it for 15 minutes without someone having to guide you through it.

EXERCISE

- Set a timer on your phone for 15 minutes and find a comfortable place to sit. It's important to be in such a position that you can be relaxed but not in such a way that you could fall asleep. Sitting cross-legged on a cushion is the most popular way but is certainly not the only way. You could sit on a chair with your feet flat on the floor and your back straight rather than leaning back. You could even lie down on the floor if you prefer, but if you do you need a way of preventing yourself from falling asleep. You can do this by putting your feet flat against the floor and your knees hip-width apart; that way should you begin to drop off, your knees will fall together and should keep you awake.

- Allow your chin to drop slightly and either close your eyes or find a comfortable spot in front of you to hold your gaze. Allow your eyes to defocus as you relax if you like.

EXERCISE

- Start by being aware of your breathing. Notice how the temperature in your nose may change as you breathe in, for example. As you take your thoughts to your breathing, make sure that you breathe deeply and efficiently, right from the bottom of your lungs and push your tummy out with each breath.

- Begin to notice that the gaps in between the in-breath and the out-breath get slightly longer. Once you've narrowed your concentration down you can expand it slightly.

- Notice any sensations, such as the way your clothes feel against your skin or the weight of your jewellery.

- If you feel that you need to move or scratch an itch, it's a good idea to pause before you do so. Once you become aware that you need to move, just wait for a moment or two and take a few more deep breaths first. It gives you a small window between what you're experiencing and your responses, which is a great skill to have.

EXERCISE

- If your mind wanders off, whether for five seconds or five minutes, just accept that it did and bring your attention back to your breathing, before expanding your focus onto any sensations again.

- Repeat this over and over again without judgement, and with no expectations until the time is up.

- When the time is up, open your eyes or lift your gaze and take a moment to notice any sounds in your environment. Notice how your body feels. Notice your thoughts or emotions.

- Rest for a moment or two and decide how you'd like to continue with the rest of your day.

As well as what you might think of as formal mindfulness, you can also utilise mindfulness more informally by focusing your attention on the day-to-day experiences you have. This is called single-tasking, which involves doing one thing at a time and giving it your full attention. As you eat your breakfast, drink a cup of tea, or walk down the street, slow it down if you can and become more aware of what you're doing. See if you can use all of your senses. A popular technique is to try and find as many things from as many senses as you can to experience in the moment.

EXERCISE

INFORMAL MINDFULNESS EXERCISE

- No matter what you're doing, go through all of your senses one by one. There's no rush though – take your time.

- Start by deliberately bringing your attention to the things that you can hear; it could be the sound of your breathing, your stomach gurgling or traffic noise outside. You might begin to notice subtle sounds that you didn't notice before.

- Then find things that you can smell. Move your attention to your environment and smell what's around you. It might be your deodorant that you notice or coffee brewing somewhere; it doesn't matter what it is. It could be the kitchen bin for all it matters, because it's the process of focusing your attention on something that improves your brain functions.

- Continue this for the other senses. What can you feel? What can you see? What can you taste? You'd be surprised how many flavours you normally delete from your meal because you don't notice that they're there.

One of the most commonly used techniques to introduce mindfulness to people is with a single raisin. At a training course I was on, we were asked to examine a raisin closely, noticing all of its wrinkles, lumps and bumps. Then we all had to close our eyes and feel the raisin between a finger and a thumb, to roll it around and become aware of all those textures. We then had to listen to it, which struck me as odd, but when I put it close to my ear and rolled it around between finger and thumb as before, I was able to ignore the feeling of the raisin against my skin for a few moments and instead was able to bring my attention to all the noises that it made as I rolled it around. Then the instructor asked us to smell it. Again, a very odd experience; I'd never sniffed a raisin before and it smells different to what you'd expect. We'd all been handling this tiny raisin for about three to four minutes before he finally asked us to put it in our mouths and begin to taste it. We weren't allowed to chew it yet, just taste it. We rolled it around our mouths, noticing that depending on where it was in our mouths it tasted slightly different. It was about then that I realised that I don't actually like raisins that much, but I'd never noticed before. I was so used to stuffing them in my mouth that I'd never really noticed what they actually taste like. We were eventually allowed to eat the raisin, and then could consume the rest of a box mindlessly if we wanted to throughout the course of the day. Which I did. And it taught me an important lesson: to be aware of what I was experiencing as there's so much more to notice if we just paid attention.

Journal Suggestions

1. What are the most unforgettable times in your life?

2. Make a list of things that inspire you.

3. What activities or hobbies would you miss if you were unable to do them?

4. What would you do if you knew you would die tonight?

5. Who has done something recently that has made your life easier and how can you thank them?

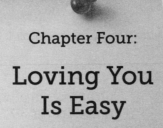

Chapter Four:

Loving You Is Easy

Self-Esteem

What is self-esteem? Put simply, self-esteem is your opinion of yourself.

Good self-esteem means that you know that you're not perfect, that no one is really, but that it doesn't matter.

It helps you to move on after making mistakes and gives you the strength to make difficult decisions.

Poor self-esteem, where your opinion of yourself is low, prevents you from moving on after mistakes and creates a lack of trust in your ability to make decisions.

Because of this, those with high self-esteem are more likely to apply for more jobs, increasing their chances of moving on in their career. They're more likely to see that their rejections are just a part of life and move on.

Someone with low self-esteem may not even bother applying for another job because "no one would want me anyway". This means that they sometimes get stuck in a job that they hate, which creates anxiety or depression.

The same thing can be said for relationships, which can allow someone with low self-esteem to be taken advantage of or abused.

The problem is that we may not even realise that our self-esteem is low because we tend to normalise our thoughts and behaviours.

MEASURING SELF-ESTEEM

So, have a look at the following statements and see to what extent you agree with them. As with the happiness test from earlier, use the following scale and give each statement a number from 1 to 6.

1 = strongly disagree
2 = moderately disagree
3 = slightly disagree
4 = slightly agree
5 = moderately agree
6 = strongly agree

1. I find it difficult to hear criticism about myself. __6__
2. I do not feel that I'm a person of worth, other people are more important. __1__
3. I tend to magnify my mistakes and ignore my successes. __5__
4. I feel that I have a number of bad qualities. __4__
5. I am easily embarrassed. __5__
6. All in all, I am inclined to feel that I am a failure. __1__

7. I often compare myself to others. __5__
8. My achievements in life have been mostly due to good luck. __1__
9. I often make decisions on the basis of what would please others without even considering my own needs. __2__
10. I rely on the opinion of others to make decisions. __2__

(32)

The lower the score (ideally below 30), the better. If you disagree with many of those statements and are actually quite comfortable in accepting yourself just the way you are, then you more than likely have quite good self-esteem. If you feel as equally entitled as anyone else to take up room on this planet and enjoy the pleasures that life can bring, then any changes you make from now on will be built on a solid foundation that will take you from strength to strength. Great news.

But, if you agree with a majority of these statements and score higher than 40, then you more than likely have quite low self-esteem. If you feel that your true self is in some way inadequate or inferior; if your thoughts are plagued by uncertainty and self-doubt; if your thoughts about yourself are often overly critical and unkind; or if you have difficulty in recognising your true worth and cannot see that you are just as entitled to the good things in life as everyone else is, then these are signs that your self-esteem is very low.

Retake this questionnaire periodically over the next few months, especially after finishing this book, and see if you've made a difference to how you view yourself.

Self-esteem underpins a lot of the ideas throughout this book – if you don't think that you deserve to be happy, then that belief will hold you back from fully engaging with these ideas. If this is you, then you need to accept that your inner critic is wrong. As you implement the suggestions I make, if a part of you is trying to hold you back because of self-doubt, remind yourself that it's just old programming – bad habits – and you're going to do it anyway. Treat yourself with the same level of respect that you'd treat someone else with.

If a friend told you that they weren't as happy in life as they know it is possible to be and that they want to do something about it, you'd be pleased for them. If they told you that they're not sure if it's fair on everyone else that they spend time looking after themselves, that it seems selfish to want to be happier, you'd challenge it. You'd tell them that they do deserve to be happy and to hell with people who think you're selfish for wanting to improve yourself. Be that encouraging friend for yourself as you progress through life and challenge that inner critic in your head when it tries to hold you back.

Putting Yourself First

Have you ever said "Yes" to something, when in your head you're screaming "Nooooo!"? Maybe you fit in with the attitude that: "If you want to get something done, ask a busy person." After all, that's what people say isn't it? But, why is that? Is that because busy people are good at getting things done? Or is it that the majority of busy people are only busy because they find it difficult to say no to people? Because it's quite hard to say no, isn't it?

We want to be compliant; we want to be liked. But it can go a bit far when we're constantly being taken advantage of. It damages our self-esteem, our belief in ourselves. It's one thing for others to see us as a bit of a soft touch, but eventually we begin to think that way about ourselves, and see ourselves as weak. Not only do we begin to resent others, but we also then start to dislike ourselves! Now, we're obviously not born this way – we're born a blank canvas as far as opinions are concerned. So what happens, as we grow, that changes us, that allows others to take advantage?

In most of my clients, it seems to be a way of preventing emotional pain. We compare the pain in having to comply with the pain of being thought of as unhelpful, and compliance wins. But, in order for compliance to win we have to exaggerate the negative possibilities in saying no, making assumptions that the other person will think of us as unfriendly or unreliable.

As with many issues that my clients present to me, they usually have an initial event or even a group of them that causes this fear of pain. The brain learns that if you're ever in the same situation again, you have to make sure you stay safe, and the brain will create anxiety about it. So, why have anxiety about saying no? Who's the anxiety really about? Is it really that person who stands over your desk with extra work for you? Or is it just the same brain circuitry that connected up when you were confronted by a bully at school? Or even a bully at home? Or earlier in your career?

There may be those initial sensitising events, but the reason the brain is still firing off the anxiety response all these years later isn't because it started. It's because it didn't stop.

The anxiety belongs in the past, and the person who's

putting pressure on you now to do something that you don't feel you should do, is different.

Recognise that saying no will not collapse your universe; it won't make someone hate you.

TIPS FOR SAYING NO

- Eye contact. A lot of people struggle with eye contact, but someone is far less likely to try and grind you down and change your mind if you can look at them in the eye as you say, "No, sorry. I can't help you today, I'm too busy." If you struggle with making eye contact, a simple trick is to look at their forehead, their nose or between their eyes instead.

- Find an alternative. If it's appropriate, you can avoid coming across as unhelpful by making a suggestion of something you could say yes to. For example "Sorry, no. Taking part in a muddy obstacle course for charity is not my idea of fun or even a source of pride, but I'm happy to set up a JustGiving donation page for you if you'd like me to help?"

EXERCISE

- Lie. A little white lie to a cold caller isn't going to do any harm. If someone knocks on your door to try and talk you into buying new windows, tell them that it's not your house, that you're renting it. Low self-esteem is often accompanied by a fear of what others think of you, so if you know that you've been polite and not flat out rejected someone who is just trying to do their job, then you've come from a place that's respectful. It gives you further evidence that you're a decent person.

- Come right out with it. There are times when just saying "No, thank you" is enough. Don't lie and say "I'll think about it" to going on holiday with someone if you know full well that you won't, because it will make you feel worse every time you see them.

One of the interesting shortcuts that our brain has evolved is the ability to feel emotional pain and physical pain in the same way. In neuroscience, there is a phrase for this: "What fires together, wires together." And usually that means that if I showed you a picture of Justin Bieber every 20 minutes and poked you in the eye each time I did so, you'd eventually find your eye watering when you saw the picture even before you were poked. But what it also means is that anytime you are fearful of something and then physically hurt by it, eventually the brain uses just the one area for both processes. If you're interested, it's the dorsal posterior insula, just above your ears and the operculo-insular region above and behind your ears.

A study that inflicted a pain stimulus on one group of test subjects in fMRI machines while another group of test subjects were shown photos of their ex-partners shortly after being dumped,[28] showed that the brain processes emotional pain in the same way as physical pain, and this seems to be particularly strong when it comes to being rejected. This makes sense when you think about it. Physical pain is a signal that there is a threat to the body, and the pain of rejection signals a threat to social bonds. Both are threats to our survival. We may like to think we are totally self-sufficient, but, as I've said before, how long would we really last out there on our own in the wild.

So, when your partner gives you the silent treatment as punishment because you came home late, it actually hurts. Everyone's been on the receiving end of it, even if it was just the idiot at school who would pretend you weren't there and say, "Did you hear something?" if you spoke. The thing is, because our response to pain is the fight or flight mechanism, it can just as easily make us angry as make us want to run away and hide. It goes some way to explain why out of 15 school shootings between 1995 and 2001, acute or chronic rejection was present in all but two of the incidents.[29]

You might not think that this is important. But understanding your emotions, gaining insight into why you feel the way you do is vital in overcoming your fear of emotion. Once you no longer fear negative emotions and can simply accept them as part of being human, you can begin doing things you wouldn't normally do, such as saying no and acting in ways that show that you're not going to be walked over.

It's not unusual for someone with low self-esteem to become a doormat to a lot of people. Good friends often get overlooked as the manipulative friends take up your time, and so there may be people that you need to start distancing yourself from. It can be hard to do this because it leaves you open to criticism, something that people with low self-esteem try to avoid at all costs. But criticism is a part of life. One thing that you can pretty much guarantee is that you will come under fire at some point. You WILL be criticised by someone, whether that's a teacher, a parent, a colleague or a random person on Facebook. We can't please everybody.

And sometimes it's because not everyone wants to be pleased in the first place. Some people actually enjoy being offended or even outraged!

So many things are taken out of context in the media for no purpose other than to give someone a reason to be angry. It's a strange quirk of human nature that negative emotions become desirable to some people.

But there's always another perspective. If someone doesn't

notice that you're behind them and lets the door close in your face, it's not because of you. When someone goes to the bar to buy eight drinks but comes back with seven and yours is the one that's missing, it's not because of you.

In extreme cases, you might get a text from a selfish friend or relative saying, "We need to talk about something that's been bothering me," when all they want to do is deliberately make you feel guilty over something pointless so that you can babysit next weekend or lend them your holiday home for a month.

It's no reflection on you.

Maybe you can get them to look at it from your perspective. If someone is criticising you over something, ask them why it is such an issue? What is it specifically that you did that is so bad?

This can help them to challenge their thought processes and maybe open up the possibility of compromise.

If a manager is standing over you with a stack of work wanting to pass the buck, you may have to keep saying, "I'm not able to do that until Tuesday, it will have to wait." Even if you have to repeat yourself over and over again.

Even if you're feeling nervous (who wouldn't?), keep your body language confident; if you stare at the floor with your shoulders hunched over then you may as well be saying "Treat me like a doormat."

But if you stand up straight, with your shoulders back a little and maintain some level of eye contact, then you're in a far better position to avoid being treated unfairly.

The key to eye contact is to not be too 'starey' but not be too shifty.

Another thing that's helpful is to agree with them in

some way, to find the common ground. If someone is having a go at you or criticising you, then it's OK to admit that you made a mistake if you did. You could agree with the truth of it, at least.

If that doesn't feel right, then agree with the odds and go with something like, "You may be right," or "There might be some truth in that." This way, you're not being defensive but you're not fully agreeing with them. Looking for ways to agree with what they say is a great way of taking constructive criticism on board.

But don't react right away. If they're standing right in front of you, take a deep breath and listen to what they're saying first rather than trying to jump in and defend yourself.

If it's an email or a social network post, then wait before you reply. Be the bigger person. If someone's being mean on social media, you don't need to criticise them back, even if you are thinking what a jerk they are.

If someone makes a nasty reply to one of your Facebook posts you can say, "I guess everyone's got different views, thanks for yours," or "It takes a lot of confidence to speak your mind, I've got to admire that, thank you."

It often means that anything that comes afterwards is far more likely to be polite, or at least less aggressive.

EXERCISE

SELF-ESTEEM TIP

Make an inventory of strengths vs weaknesses.

- Divide a piece of paper in half and write 'Strengths' as a heading on one half.

- On the opposite half, write 'Weaknesses'.

- List ten strengths that you have in the first column and ten weaknesses in the other.

- It doesn't matter how small you might perceive those strengths to be; after all, somebody with low self-esteem is likely to pick up on the most minuscule of weaknesses, so do the same for your strengths.

- If you need some help with your strengths, start the sentence with, "I was proud of myself when...". See what pops into your mind, no matter how small, to complete the sentence.

It can be a long process to boost your confidence, but it starts with being good to yourself. So, treat yourself with the same level of respect that you'd give to someone else. Imagine you're having a drink with a friend and they knock over their drink. What would you say? Would you call them an idiot? Would you spend ten minutes telling them how useless they were? I'd hope not.

But, what if it was you that knocked over a drink? Would you call yourself an idiot? Would you spend ten minutes telling yourself how useless you are? It can be hard to override the inner critic, but your inner advocate can be louder – it just takes a bit of practice. It's a bit like having a devil on one shoulder and an angel on the other.

If your inner dialogue can start being supportive, then it will become habitual not to put yourself down at every opportunity. Even if you don't believe it at first, imagine that you are 'worth it'. In what way would your life be different?

Would you eat healthier? Exercise? Do more things that you enjoy doing?

Once you have an awareness of what you're doing wrong and what you should be doing instead, it's going to be easier to recognise that your thoughts and emotions can be habitual. The best way to override old habits like this and replace them with new ones is to repeat something every day until it becomes second nature.

Is there something that you've been doing every day that reminds you that you aren't worthy? Maybe you need to stop comparing yourself to other people. Social media has a lot to answer for here. We can't mind-read, so we don't really know how happy someone is with their life, and looking through Facebook and assuming that every friend you have is happier, richer and more popular than you is like creating a fictitious universe in your head.

What someone else shows you about their life is usually very much filtered. You may only see what they want you to see.

In the modern age, self-esteem may be perceived differently by each person. One person might say that they base how they think about themselves by how much money they have, while another may say that it's the way that they look, and another may think it's how popular they are.

The happy characters will often say that none of those make a difference to their self-esteem, and they judge themselves on whether they are fulfilling their purpose in life, even if that purpose is simply to read good books and watch good movies.

So if someone else has a different view of self-esteem and is trying to make themselves feel better by creating the perfect life on Facebook, take it with a pinch of salt!

Labels

Do you have any labels?

Labels are important, both in terms of the way we label ourselves and the way the world around you labels you. So think for a moment – do you have a label? Whether that's about your personality, your behaviour or even your job. Do other people label you?

I think of myself as a relatively nice guy, and I'd help anyone in trouble because, for whatever reason, as a youngster, I labelled myself as someone people could trust, one of the good guys.

I remember being quite young – ten years old maybe – and walking back from the supermarket with my mum one Saturday afternoon. We had one particularly heavy shopping bag, and so we held on to a handle each as we walked the three-quarters of a mile or so back home. On the way there, we bumped into someone my mum knew and she made some flattering comment about me, which at the time I took to mean that I was helpful. It felt good to be appreciated; being liked pushes some safety buttons in the brain and reminds us that we aren't being rejected. The fact that I remember it means a part of me must have in some way fixated on it, creating an association in the brain with reward, so that I was always on the lookout for another reason to be liked or appreciated and therefore not rejected. And if you look hard enough and often enough for anything, you'll find it. So I found lots of opportunities over the years to be thought of as helpful and trustworthy. I acted that way until it became my identity, my personality. But it came at a cost.

Fixating on the concept of being thought of as helpful meant that being thought of as unhelpful pushed the scary buttons. Being judged became the worst thing in the world to me. As a youngster, it didn't really cause an issue because there wasn't a great deal of pressure to be helpful. In most situations, teachers and parents will look out for us to ensure that we don't get taken advantage of. But what happens when we start looking after ourselves?

I'll tell you what happened to me. I had a problem saying no. I associated being helpful with being liked and associated being liked with being safe. So if someone was to ring me up and ask me to drop everything for them, I would have. Eventually I became aware that I was easy to take advantage of and began to say no but it was difficult. It meant overriding my core beliefs about myself, the one thing that kept me safe. And it's still hard all these years later, but being aware of what makes me tick means that I can be more honest with myself in those situations. Knowing that I associate positive emotion and being seen as helpful means that I examine my decisions a little closer. I query why I feel the urge to say, "Sure, I can help," to see if I genuinely do want to help or not. As a therapist, it can be very tempting to take on every client that contacts me for help, even the ones that say, "But I can only see you after work – do you see clients after 6pm?" So I do need to practise what I preach and learn to say no sometimes. It begins to override the original label I gave myself that said "Can't Say No" on it.

Unfortunately the way the brain works means that labels are important. Our brain has the ability to make shortcuts to make it more efficient, and labelling is one of the things that it does to make our lives easier. It makes stereotypes that we already have an opinion about to save us having to think. We all do it to others and others will do it to us, so we sometimes get given the wrong labels based on someone else's preconceived ideas. But we don't have to stick these labels onto ourselves. Being aware that people make mistakes is vital in order to recognise that we have the freedom whether or not to react to their labelling.

Let me tell you about a couple of clever experiments.

In one study,[30] students at Princeton University were asked to judge the academic performance of a girl named Hannah. They were given a handout with a short biography about her life and were asked to watch two videos. One showed her school and her playing in her local area, and a second video showed her answering questions designed to assess things such as her ability with mathematics, science, reading and social skills. Afterwards, they were asked to decide whether Hannah had performed below average, above average or spot on for a Year 5 student. But the video of her answering questions was put together in such a way that made it difficult to tell; she would sometimes answer tricky questions easily and sometimes she would seem a little distracted and make mistakes over easier questions.

The study was designed to confuse anyone watching and leave them without an accurate picture of her abilities. The only way to form an opinion of them was to go to the only other information they had about her, and that was the label they stuck on her when watching the very first introductory video and reading the handout. Now, here's the interesting bit. Half of the students had seen footage of her playing in an attractive, tree-lined park. Her neighbourhood was a suburban environment set on landscaped grounds with six-bedroomed houses. Her school was large and spacious with great sports facilities, which suggested that her family was wealthy. The biography said that her parents were college-educated with great jobs. Her dad was an attorney and her mum a freelance writer.

Meanwhile, the other students saw the different video and had a different handout. To them, Hannah was playing in a stark, fenced-in schoolyard. Her neighbourhood was an urban environment with tiny, run-down houses. Her school was small and cramped and suggested it was poor. This time the biography said that her parents hadn't gone to college, only high school. Her dad was a meat packer and her mum worked from home as a seamstress.

So, how much of an influence did the two videos have on opinions of her academic abilities? Well the answer is a big one! Those that thought she came from a wealthy background rated her abilities well above average for her age, whereas those that thought she came from a lower-class background rated her abilities as below average. The interesting thing is that both groups were able to explain why they made their decision. Both groups found evidence in the testing video that proved their existing opinion. They had labelled her from the start. They'd already made their mind up, and when watching the video footage of the testing, all it did was confirm their existing beliefs.

This is why it's rare for the super-successful types in business to come from a lower-class background. In a survey of 265 chief executive officers (CEOs) of various US corporations, Jennifer Kish-Gephart, assistant professor of management in the Sam M. Walton College of Business, and Joanna Campbell at the University of Cincinnati, found that CEOs with lower-class origins made up only 3.4% of the total. When interviewed, 38.5% said they were from a lower-middle background, 38.1% said middle class, 17% responded with upper-middle class and 3% labelled their origins as upper class.

Out of those that make it into higher management, we also see a difference in how much they earn. A 2016 study by Professor Sam Friedman of the London School of Economics and Professor Daniel Laurison of Swarthmore College in Pennsylvania, showed that top-level managers who were highly qualified, but who thought of themselves as being born into a lower class, were paid less. Many said they felt less entitled to ask for pay rises and even exclude themselves from seeking promotion because of anxieties about fitting in.

The average annual salary of someone in high-level management whose parents were also in high-level management was £50,519, but this dropped to £44,338 if their parents were only in lower supervisory positions. The statistics drop further as their parents' careers were lower down the ladder, with the managers whose parents were unemployed averaging £38,748. This is almost £12k less than the managers with parents also in high-level management, despite the fact that both had the same qualifications and performed the same role. All because of these labels that either other people stick on us or the labels we give ourselves.

When it comes to these labels, we can create positive ones, such as strong, confident, proud, happy, enthusiastic, graceful or bright. Or we can create negative ones, including awkward, stupid, weak, incapable, ugly, poor or greedy.

PULLING OFF YOUR LABELS

Here's a little exercise that may help you to identify your labels and replace them with something more helpful. If you've already been practising meditation, you may find it easier. It's a technique I use with hypnotherapy clients and involves mental relaxation as a way of distracting your conscious thoughts. This allows us to gain a better understanding of where our mental programming comes from and get a better perspective on it.

EXERCISE

- Find somewhere to relax, close your eyes and take a few deep breaths.

- Take your thoughts to the tips of your toes and imagine that even the tiniest of muscles there are softening and relaxing.

- Move up through your feet and ankles and imagine that they too are letting go of tension.

- Work your way up through your body, imagining how it would feel as each part of you is relaxing. All the way to the top of your head.

- Now that your body is relaxing, it's going to be easier to relax your mind, so begin to capture your attention. Take your thoughts away somewhere, anywhere. Maybe a place you've visited or somewhere you've just created in your daydreams that feels engaging or enjoyable. You could even be riding a bike in a race. It's the process of capturing your attention that's important, not necessarily how you do it.

EXERCISE

- Now that you've begun the process of mental relaxation, you can begin to use your imagination to your advantage. So whatever you're doing in your imagination, begin to change it, by imagining that some sort of doorway appears, if there isn't already one there. It could be a real door or a science-fiction portal that transports you to another world.

- Walk through this doorway and allow the previous daydream to fade away as you find yourself standing at the back of a room. This room has nothing in it but a full-length mirror at the other end of it.

- Walk over to the mirror, and as you get closer to it you realise that it's a magic mirror that allows you to see things you wouldn't normally be able to see.

- Once up close to this mirror it shows you that there is a sticky label stuck on your chest, a label that has something written on it, maybe just a

EXERCISE

single word. It could say "Stupid" or "Unworthy". Or it might have a short sentence written on it. This magic mirror might show your reflection reversed but it shows the words to you the correct way round.

- As you stand in front of this mirror you look at your chest to see where the label would be, but it's invisible. You can only see the label in your reflection, but now you know where it is.

- Imagine reaching for the label on your chest and begin pulling it off.

- Look into the mirror and imagine yourself peeling the label from your chest.

- Once you've pulled it off, you notice that the words on the label begin to fade and eventually disappear.

- As it does this, the label begins to appear in your hand outside of the mirror too.

EXERCISE

- This is a magical world, where anything can happen and so you can write a new word or sentence on this blank label with your finger. You can't see the writing unless you look in the mirror, and when you look, the writing is the correct way round and easy to read as you stick this new label onto your chest again, maybe in a different place.

- Perhaps underneath the original label, there are more labels underneath for you to peel off. If so, peel them off and watch the words disappear as you then rewrite them attaching new labels to yourself.

- Once you've rid yourself of your old labels and replaced them with new ones, you can turn away from the mirror and walk back the way you came, before taking a few deep breaths and opening your eyes.

Another collection of experiments[31] that's worth understanding was undertaken by a social psychologist named Mark Snyder who set up some ten-minute phone calls with 51 men and women. Before the call took place though, the man was shown a photograph supposedly of the woman he'd be talking to, but it wasn't. The picture was one of two pictures that had been chosen from a previous study of a woman that was classed as either attractive or unattractive. The phone calls were recorded to review later on and the man was asked to give his impression of what the woman was like to talk to. Not surprisingly, the women that were supposedly more attractive were described more positively. The men had labelled the women before the call was even made and a bias of 'beautiful people are good people' led them to a particular opinion.

But here's the bit that tickles me. The recordings were used in a later study by having people listen to the recordings looking for evidence of this bias in the conversations. They were asked to listen for examples of things like flirtatiousness, enthusiasm and friendliness. And what they found is that the women who, without even knowing they were being perceived by the men as physically attractive, actually spoke in a more flirtatious and likeable way. The women who were being thought of as unattractive were less friendly and more cold or aloof.

It transpires that the way the man had labelled the woman right at the start changed the way that he treated her in conversation, and she responded accordingly. It shows that if you think of someone in a negative way, it actually brings out their negative qualities, and vice versa. If you think of someone in a positive way, you'll treat them in such a way as to bring out the positive traits to their personality.

This is important stuff; it's why so many times you hear of people wanting to split up with someone because the spark in their partner's personality has gone, and so they fall out of love with them and the couple break up. Afterwards, they will no doubt notice that their ex has become exactly the sort of person that they find attractive again. Now that their real personality isn't being held back, their ex suddenly becomes the lively, enthusiastic, flirtatious and attractive person that was always there in the first place, and they're desperate to get back with them so that they can drink piña coladas and get caught in the rain. Rupert Holmes clearly new what he was talking about in his song 'Escape', and his story is probably not that far-fetched.

Probably the most famous experiment to show the effects of labelling people was undertaken in the 1960s by Harvard psychologist Robert Rosenthal and Lenore Jacobson, the principal of Spruce Elementary School in South San Francisco.[32]

Jacobson had been intrigued by an experiment that Rosenthal had carried out at Harvard University in which he had tricked researchers into believing that certain rats had been genetically bred to be either very good or very bad at finding their way through mazes. Actually the rats were just plain old rats and no genetic modification had taken place at all. The researchers were told that the experiment was simply to give them some experience at handling rats, and they were instructed to teach each rat (the 'genetically modified' ones and the 'regular' ones) how to take food from one area of the maze to another. Amazingly, because of the expectations of the researchers about the abilities of the two 'different' types of rats, the rats did indeed become either very good or very bad at finding their way through mazes. This is called the Experimenter Expectancy Effect, and is why in experiments nowadays, even with drug trials, no one knows what to expect from a participant. If ever you take part in any drug trials, even your doctor won't know whether you're taking a placebo or not.

Rosenthal wrote about this expectancy effect in a 1963 article in *American Scientist*. In it, he hypothesised that, "If rats became brighter when expected to, then it should not be far-fetched to think that children could become brighter when expected to by their teachers."

This prompted Jacobson to write to him. "If you ever 'graduate' to classroom children," she wrote, "please let me know whether I can be of assistance." Rosenthal got in touch with her faster than a hungry rat runs through a maze.

Together they devised a way of replicating the rat experiment, but with an entire school of children aged between five and ten.

The Spruce School teachers were all told that every child was to be given a fancy-titled new test called 'The Harvard Test of Inflected Acquisition'. They were told that the test was to identify which of the children were the 'academic bloomers', the children that would show great academic improvement over the following year. But it wasn't.

The fancy test was in fact nothing more than a collection of standard IQ tests, specific to each age group, which did nothing other than indicate how smart the children were at that specific point, and certainly wouldn't identify how much of an improvement they'd be able to predict over the following year at all. The tests were marked and scores for each child were kept to one side for later. Some had performed below expectations for their age, some above and some scored spot on.

Then comes the controversial part of the experiment. At random, 20% of the children were picked out of the list, and assigned the title of an academic bloomer. The average IQ for this 20% was the same as the entire school as a whole, so some were below average, some above, some spot on. But there was nothing at all to indicate any future success in their academic qualities. So, all the teachers in the school were given a list of names and were told to expect great things from these children. They were told that over the next 12 months, these children would experience quite a rapid period of intellectual growth. The year trundled on and soon the children were moved up to the next year and were given a new teacher, a teacher with an expectation.

This expectation meant that at the end of the school year, when all the children took the IQ test again, 80% of the so-called 'bloomers' had a minimum of a ten-point improvement in their IQ. By contrast, only 50% of the other children showed any such improvement on the test.

These random names on a list created a change in the way that each child was taught. Because the teachers 'knew' that a child was in some way gifted, they were more patient with them and overlooked their mistakes as just part of the 'blooming' process. Every time they did well, the teachers praised them and encouraged the blooming that they knew was coming. It was subtle but it made a huge difference to the children.

Rosenthal called his discovery 'The Pygmalion Effect', after the mythological Greek sculptor whose love for an ivory statue of a woman he created was so great that it came to life. You might be more familiar with the play it eventually inspired, George Bernard Shaw's *Pygmalion*, and its musical version, *My Fair Lady*. In these productions, Professor Henry Higgins makes over the Cockney flower girl Eliza Doolittle, bringing forth my two favourite quotes of all time: "Happy is the man who can make a living by his hobby" from the original *Pygmalion* and a line that featured in both versions: "The difference between a lady and a flower girl is not how she behaves, but how she's treated." I try to live my life by those quotes, but the latter in particular, because we will never see the best in someone if we're treating them like their worst.

What does your name say about you?

Here's something interesting for you. Did you know that having a name that sounds a little bit like the word 'dentist', such as Denise or Dennis means that you are more likely to become a dentist than if you're called Brian?

And also that having a surname that begins with an early letter of the alphabet, such as A, B or C leads to greater confidence and success in life than if your surname starts with X, Y or Z.

But why?

Well, the first is a concept known as 'nominative determinism', a term coined by *New Scientist* after observing that the subject matter of a series of science books and articles bore relevance to the authors' surnames. The idea for the concept started when one of the editors of *New Scientist* was sent a paper on incontinence in the

British Journal of Urology which was written by J W Splatt and D Weedon.

And, after glancing around at his own collection of books, the editor came across a book on the Arctic called *Pole Positions: The Polar Regions and the Future of the Planet*, by Daniel Snowman.

Following this, research was undertaken and a paper was written about this phenomenon entitled 'Why Susie Sells Seashells by the Seashore: Implicit Egotism and Major Life Decisions' and was published in the *Journal of Personality and Social Psychology*.[33]

It concluded that people indeed are disproportionately likely to choose careers whose labels resemble their names.

Further research[34] even found that there are more couples that share the same surname initial than is predicted by chance, as if we are drawn towards a partner simply because of their surname reminding us of our own.

As for what's called 'alphabetical discrimination', where we are more likely to be successful in life if our name is called out early in the school register, the most significant research was conducted a few years ago with help from 15,000 readers of the *Daily Telegraph*. These readers logged on to the newspaper's website and answered questions about various aspects of their lives. After the answers were analysed, it was found that readers whose surnames began with letters at the beginning of the alphabet did indeed rate themselves as significantly more successful overall than those with surnames starting with end-of-the-alphabet initials. The most significant difference was in career success.

From a therapist's perspective, I can understand how this would happen. Beliefs about self often start at school, and because we associate the top of a list with winners and the bottom with losers, it would easily impact on self-esteem if you were drip-fed the knowledge that there are more people above you in life.

So, if these subtleties influence the way we perceive ourselves throughout our lives without even knowing it, just how much difference can we make to ourselves if we did something less subtle to change the way we think about ourselves? How much better could you feel if you actually made a decision today to intentionally change and began taking steps to do it?

Well, congratulations! Because that's exactly what you are doing – that's the whole point of this book. And, in taking these steps to be a happier version of you, you now know that you need to be careful how you label yourself and others, because it really does influence how we experience the world.

Maybe spend some time thinking about the labels and expectations that have been put on you throughout your life and see if you're playing a role that you don't want to play any more.

Carrot Or Stick?

What's the best way to make a donkey go faster? Is it to give it a carrot or is it to hit it with a stick?

I won't lie to you – I don't actually know and I'm not going to go and hit some donkeys in order to find out. But my assumptions are that hitting it with a stick would work in the short term and giving it a carrot would work in the long term. After all, the best way to keep something healthy is definitely to feed it rather than beat it.

I mention this because it's very common to beat ourselves up, rather than give ourselves support, but we need to treat ourselves with respect, without judgement.

Do you ever find yourself saying these sorts of phrases to yourself?

"You're useless."

"Don't even bother, you'll only screw it up."

"Look at the state of you, you ugly lump of lardy cake."

It's hard to see how these sorts of statements would help, isn't it? The only way that sort of self-talk would motivate you to improve yourself is if you were able to counter attack it.

Attack: "You're useless."

Counterattack: "I've got room for improvement, yes, and I'm willing to learn."

Attack: "Don't even bother, you'll only screw it up."

Counterattack: "But I'll never know unless I try."

Attack: "Look at the state of you, you ugly lump of lardy cake."

Counterattack: "What the hell's lardy cake?"

You get the idea.

Our inner voice isn't any sign of mental illness – we all have an internal dialogue that runs throughout our entire day. Sometimes it's supportive, but sometimes it really isn't, and if you've got into a habit of having a very critical inner voice, it might be time to do something about it.

It's important not to argue with your inner critic, but the fact that it exists means there is some belief system at play here.

And just shouting at yourself in a cyclical tirade of "No I'm not", "Yes you are", "No I'm not", "Yes you are", isn't much use. If a part of you is telling you that you're stupid, then a part of you believes that you are, and pretending that it isn't there is simply burying your head in the sand.

Listen to whose voice it is. Is it your own voice? Or is it someone else's? Many clients of mine have spoken about their internal dialogue, and so often it's an overly critical parent that they hear or a bullying teacher.

Listen to what your inner critic says because it will help you understand more about your fears. There may be some benefit to these negative bombardments because often this inner voice is trying to protect you from getting hurt in some way. What does holding you back from doing something achieve? If your inner voice is trying to hold you back from applying for a new job because "You won't get it anyway!", ask yourself, "What's so bad about that?" See what comes up, because it could be that your anxieties are in a different place to where you think they are.

In the case of the inner voice holding someone back from applying for a new job, it might not be a fear of the interview that needs working on; it could be the fear of disappointment. So spending time working on your ability to handle job interviews wouldn't quiet the inner critic very much at all. Instead you'd need to work on your emotional strength and your resilience. Talk yourself into having faith that the only way to learn how to handle disappointment is to experience it and move on from it.

Once you've got a better understanding of what the inner voice really means, you may find that the pain it's trying to protect you from relates to something from your past,

ur present. Understanding some of the origins of our
urities can be very helpful at getting a better perspective
on them, so that the past can begin to feel like the past rather
than continuing to repeat the memory of the day that you
accidentally called your teacher 'Mum'.

The best way to build yourself up if your self-esteem is
quite low is to work with those negative beliefs about self,
rather than work against them. Trying to make changes by
lying to yourself will not work, yet many self-help books will
suggest the benefits of positive affirmations. I won't name
any names, but believe me that there are dozens of books
out there that suggest because the same area of the brain we
use for imagining something is the same as for experiencing
something, then saying positive statements to yourself will
make it real if you do it enough times.

They might suggest looking in a mirror and repeating
phrases such as "You are a happy and beautiful person". Or
"I am enthusiastic and full of energy. Confidence is second
nature to me". That's fine if you already are that character
and you're using affirmations to stay that way while dealing
with something crummy that's happened in your life. But ·
in reality, most people will seek help because they don't
think that they are happy or beautiful. These affirmations
will feel empty and fake, and studies have shown they can
actually make you feel worse rather than better. Research
published in the journal *Psychological Science*[35] came to
the conclusion that "repeating positive self-statements
may benefit certain people, such as individuals with high
self-esteem, but backfire for the very people who need them
the most".

This quote came about after an experiment where people

were asked to take a self-esteem questionnaire and were asked afterwards to take part in a writing exercise for four minutes. Some of the participants were also told that when they hear a doorbell they have to repeat the phrase "I am a lovable person". After that, everyone filled out another three questionnaires that measured mood and self-esteem. What it showed was that thinking about being lovable when you don't believe you are is highly detrimental. However, people with high self-esteem felt better after repeating the positive affirmation, but only slightly.

These ideas were backed up by previous research by Donna Eisenstadt and her husband Michael Leippe[36] that showed that when people get feedback that they believe is overly positive, they actually feel worse, rather than better. I learned that the hard way a few years ago when I saw a female friend that I'd not seen for a few months and said, "Hey, you look good. Have you lost weight?" "No!" she said, "I've put some on actually." And then she ignored me for the rest of the night. If external positives can have a negative effect, then internal ones are going to feel even more fake.

QUICK SELF-ESTEEM BOOST

Take a pack of sticky notes and write yourself some encouraging messages to leave around your home or workspace. They don't need to be complicated or elaborate, but make them appropriate for you. It could be just as simple as writing the word 'smile' to remind you that you should. Or as specific as, "Don't compare myself to others. I'm perfect as I am." A nice one to leave somewhere that you will see it regularly is, "I am enough." Or, "I am a good enough (fill in the space)."

Do you need to remind yourself that you are a good enough something? What should your inner voice say that you can remind yourself of with these sticky notes? "I am a good enough son"? "I am a good enough teacher"? Or simply, "I am good enough"?

Sally

Sally was 28 when she came for therapy. On her intake form, she'd ticked nearly every issue. Alcohol, anger, anxiety, confidence, self-esteem and weight issues, among other things. In short, she was not a happy lady. Although she held herself with a defiant body language that to most people would appear as strong and self-assured, it was a defence mechanism. Behind the tattoos, the low-cut T-shirts and the assertive attitude was a woman who thought of herself as the bottom of the pile.

This attitude went way back. Sally had been brought up in a household that was highly unpredictable; both her parents were alcoholics and she would come home from school not knowing whether there would be food on the table or whether she'd get a smack in the mouth for asking, so she spent more time outside than inside. Because of this, her homework was never finished and her schoolwork suffered, as did her belief in her abilities and her expectation of her future.

The only way to get her basic needs of food and shelter met was to make friends with someone older and beg to sleep on their floor. Eventually she learnt that she could use sex as a way of convincing men that she was worth having around, and it seemed ideal at first. But shacking up with the type of man that was happy to swap sex for rent meant her life was just as toxic as the home environment she had escaped from. She would often get beaten, and when she felt strong enough to escape, she would simply run to the next toxic man, knowing that she'd be taken in by him at least. She never bothered to find a nice guy; after all, "A nice guy wouldn't want me anyway."

This pattern continued until she was 19, when she became pregnant. She waited a week before she told the man she was living with, knowing that he'd throw her out of the house or force her to have an abortion. Instead, he threw her down the stairs and kicked her in the face and stomach, breaking her nose and three ribs. It was then she realised that things needed to change.

She admitted that if she hadn't been pregnant, she probably wouldn't have gone to the hospital; after all, she believed that she "wasn't worth bothering with". As you can expect, her desire to look after her baby was greater than her desire to look after herself, and once it was confirmed at the hospital that the baby was safe, she was encouraged to get help through organisations such as Women's Aid or Refuge, which she did. The local council eventually found her a house, and she was able to begin the process of rebuilding her life.

Her priority was her baby girl and every effort went into making sure that she was safe and well. Unfortunately, putting someone else's needs before her own, even the needs of her daughter, had more and more of a negative effect upon her self-esteem.

Every baby and toddler group she took her baby girl to

made her feel more and more anxious. It was good for her daughter to be there so she stuck it out, but even in a crowded room she felt more and more alone each time she went. It wouldn't matter how nice anyone was to her – she still felt as if she didn't belong there. In her mind she was unlovable, so a part of her was on the lookout to prove her right. If two people in the room were laughing with each other, she was convinced they were laughing at her. If someone tried to chat with her, then she became suspicious that they wanted something from her as if there was an ulterior motive for someone to treat her kindly. Whenever she tried to shake herself out of this mindset, she would see that there was no reason to feel the way she did and it would instead be replaced with guilt for thinking badly of people.

Over a few years, she tried many things to feed her loneliness. She turned to alcohol, food, cigarettes. Everything made her feel worse; everything she did in her life made her feel guilty for not being a better mum. When her daughter started school, it gave her more time to feel sorry for herself. With no qualifications and no work experience, she didn't even bother looking for work, because she believed that no one would want her anyway. Her loneliness led her to meet people that would only make her feel worse, being unconsciously attracted to all the wrong types of characters. This led to more drinking, drug use and promiscuity.

It came to a head one New Year's Eve, when her daughter was injured. She was almost seven years old and was watching the fireworks on the TV while her mum had friends round. One of these so-called friends threw a glass ashtray that hit her on the back of the head, leading to a 48-hour hospital visit and five stitches. Social services then threatened to take her daughter away from her if things didn't change dramatically. It was a dreadful way to get a wake-up call, but it's exactly what Sally needed to take steps to make sure that nothing like that ever happened again.

When she came to me, she didn't really know what she wanted to achieve. She just knew that she needed to move forward in her life, forget about the past and become a better inspiration for her daughter. She'd found a job cleaning at a local garden centre and began to slowly learn to trust people enough to learn to like them. But she hated herself.

She couldn't forgive herself for putting her daughter in harm's way, and every time she saw herself reflected in a window at work she would remind herself how bad she was, how stupid, how ugly. She found it impossible to see the good in herself as the bad was so overpowering to her.

We explored many different issues during her therapy: her anger towards her family, their rejection, the foundations of her personality, her beliefs about herself. But the biggest aspect in terms of her progress was learning to respect herself.

I gave her some homework to talk to herself every day. After taking her daughter to school and before getting ready for work, she was to spend 15 minutes standing in front of a mirror and had to speak about three very specific topics. But, I asked her to do it in the second person narrative, meaning she was to talk to herself like a friend. She had been using the second person narrative all of her life, telling herself things like, "You're such a useless person" and "Everyone hates you, Sally". It was time to learn how to change.

So, I gave her three open-ended sentences to complete every day in front of her mirror. The first started with: "Sally, I'm proud that you..." It was perfectly OK to go back 20 years if she needed to – there were things in her past that needed acknowledging, accepting and moving away from – as well as talking about the things going on right now and in the recent past.

This is what she told me she'd said:

"Sally, I'm proud that you are taking steps to better yourself."

"Sally, I'm proud that you looked after your mum when she was unable to look after herself."

"Sally, I'm proud that you got out of the abusive relationships."

I asked her to expand upon each sentence in front of the mirror, and she would encourage herself by explaining to herself why she did the things she did from another person's point of view.

She did the same thing for the second sentence, which began: "Sally, I forgive you for...", which led to these responses:

"Sally, I forgive you for letting your standards in friends get so low it put yourself and your daughter in danger. I forgive you for that."

"Sally, I forgive you for seeking love and acceptance with sex, when you didn't know any other way."

"Sally, I forgive you for trying to find an escape with drugs, when all you wanted to do was forget about your life."

"Sally, I forgive you for leaving school when you had no faith in yourself to pass an exam."

Again, she expanded on her experiences to explain why she did what she did and was able to learn to let go of the past.

The third sentence was: "Sally, I commit to you that...", and she came up with:

"Sally, I commit to you that I will be there to support you. To forgive you and to love you."

"Sally, I commit to you that I will not allow your past to dictate your future."

"Sally, I commit to you that you will never need anyone else to love you more than I do."

She spoke to herself in the same way that she would do if she was encouraging her best friend. She learned to have self-respect and self-esteem.

She did this every day for six weeks, and throughout that time, she had weekly therapy sessions to talk it all through. After that, we began spacing the sessions further and further apart. Towards the end of her therapy, she was having driving lessons and had signed up at an Adult Education Centre.

At her last appointment, she told me she had applied for a different role at the garden centre and was due to have an interview the following day. She felt confident, proud and was happy to see where her life was going to go next, whether she got the job or not.

As she was leaving, she reached into her bag and took out a gift for me. It was a paperweight in the shape of a door in a frame. The door was slightly ajar and on one side was written 'One door closes', and on the opposite side it said "Another opens".

Self-esteem is a personal reflection of your sense of your own worth.

A self-judgement based on your interactions throughout life, or rather your reactions to those interactions.

These reactions can either raise or lower your self-esteem,

so if you've been reacting in a way that lowers it, then something needs to change. Remember to be nice to yourself.

Treat yourself with the same respect that you'd give someone else. Eat healthily and exercise. Do things that you enjoy doing.

MIRROR AFFIRMATIONS

It can be very helpful to use Sally's mirror exercise. Maybe you need to get in front of a mirror and spend a little time alone too.

The three sentences that you say to yourself while looking into the mirror are:

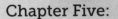

Chapter Five:

Be OK About Not Being OK

What is the perfect life?

If you look around at the world through the glossy magazines and social media updates from old school friends, it can appear as if everyone's really got it all together. And if you hadn't realised it before, I'm sure you've got the hint from me by now that it's not true. It's a lie to make you feel bad about yourself in a lame attempt to make someone else feel good. You know that already: I've said it so far in this book enough times now so I'm not going to say it again.

Things won't always go your way, and it's OK to feel upset, sad, depressed even. Life is not a continuous experience of pleasure and happiness. Sometimes bad things happen. Even happy people can have relationship problems and get divorced. Even after implementing all the ideas in this book for a few years, you might lose your job and be very fed up about it. You might even have to move house because you can't afford the payments any more. A very close friend or relative may die. Things are going to happen to you in your life that are awful. In fact, they might already have happened. It could be that you have a serious illness, mental or physical, that holds you back. You might have clinical depression, or chronic fatigue syndrome. You might have a damaged body that makes movement 1,000 times harder than it should. Sometimes life is just crap and it's OK to feel depressed about it. It's OK to have bad days, bad weeks, bad months even.

It's just important that you don't let yourself stay there forever. The longer you stay there, the worse it will get and you can feel stuck. Getting stuck in that frame of mind will only drag you down further and further.

So if you're having a bad time of it at the minute, recognise that it's OK to get it out of your system and have a good cry if you want before moving on. We need to feel sad so that we know where in our lives we need to make changes, and accept the things that we can't. We need to feel angry if we see injustice so as to know how to try and prevent it from happening again, if we can.

With many problems it's the extreme ends of our acceptance of these problems that causes our life to get worse. By that I mean that ignoring something means that it will get worse, and focusing on it means that it will get worse. By accepting what's going on, you can then work around it so as to move forward. A friend of mine recently had a motorbike accident and broke his arm. He had to have a metal plate screwed into his bones to hold them together and spent a frustrating week in hospital. Just 48 hours after coming out of the hospital, he flew off to the Isle of Man TT races and pretended it hadn't happened. An infection soon set in and within a week he became a gibbering, shivering wreck. He had to spend another week in hospital, undergoing a second operation to try and clean out the infection.

His body wasn't working properly and he should have taken it easy while it healed. That same attitude applies to mental health as well. That's no secret. If you're going through a rough patch, accept it. Don't ignore it, otherwise you won't heal.

Life is full of ups and downs and you're probably going to have some bad times. But as well as that, you're also going to have great times – experiences that make you happy and fulfilled and make the bad times all seem worthwhile.

Look at it this way. If you had an old classic car that had a few problems with it, you'd still look after it. It doesn't have power steering, so you have to work a bit harder when having to do a three-point turn. It can't go faster than 60mph, so when you drive on a motorway you have to stay in the slow lane, but you still get to where you want to go. You just need to set out a few minutes earlier than if you were driving a brand new car. It's a lovely old car – it just has a few quirks. It struggles to start on cold mornings and for some odd reason the horn will occasionally sound itself when you're turning right. Knowing that it has these quirks doesn't change the fact that it's a lovely car, so you just have to work around its problems.

I spend so much time teaching people how to be the best they can be, that it's easy to overlook how necessary it is to ensure that you don't push yourself too far when your mind or body isn't strong enough.

Clients will often come into therapy and describe their idea of a perfect personality when asking me to help them. They seek to be this strong, dynamic character, who is driven and enthusiastic. They rarely describe how they're going to relax and enjoy life, and instead perceive that in order to be a successful human being, they must be constantly busy.

Now, don't get me wrong – a busy person is often a happy person. There's lots of pride and satisfaction in life, but it has to be balanced.

I see just as many motivated clients as I do unmotivated ones; it's just that they present with different issues.

Someone who is too busy can develop severe stress and not really notice it, feeling as if they thrive on adrenaline and can't work without it.

These are often the busy mums with high-flying jobs that take part in a 10km charity race at a moment's notice before working late into the night on a business proposal, then getting up early for a meeting with the boss and going to bed late because they promised their belly dancing friend they'd support them at a show.

When describing this to unmotivated clients, they may say, "I wish I could be like that," as if it's something to strive for.

Yet too much of that sort of life can lead to a real crash in many people. It's important to learn how to say no sometimes, to be in that happy middle ground where you don't care too little about what other people might think of you, but you don't care too much. It's important to pay attention to your body, and if it's telling you that you need more rest, then you give it rest.

One of the surprising questions that I ask my clients is, "Does your alarm clock wake you up?" So many of them will say, "Yes, I'm fast asleep when it goes off." If that's the case, then they needed more sleep. If your alarm clock has to wake you, then you need to go to bed earlier. But it's so easy to find excuses as to why you can't, isn't it? Listen to the messages your body gives you – striving to be perfect can have the exact opposite effect if you don't. In extreme cases, it can create the massively debilitating condition known as ME or chronic fatigue syndrome, but before it turns into that there are plenty of signs that you're trying too hard at life.

British squash champion Peter Marshall was the world's number two player. He was 24 years old and the new season was about to start. He was at the top of his game and getting ever closer to the goal that had consumed him for years, of knocking the world number one Jansher Khan off the top spot, when the signs that something wasn't right began to appear. He developed glandular fever but carried on playing, battling through it until his body was exhausted. That's when it was diagnosed as chronic fatigue syndrome and he was told he had to take a year out. He did as he was told; bored as he was, he didn't touch a racquet for a year, and when he did it took him another two years to slowly increase his strength until he felt good enough to compete.

While recovering, he was even given the option of quitting and receiving a huge compensation payout from his insurers. But he was told that if he played just one professional match, he would forfeit the money. He took his time, recovered and became British National Champion, rocketing back into the international top ten. But it took respect for his condition to allow him to recover, and he's not the only one to have had to face it.

This can happen to anyone suffering with great emotional stress, but couple that with a competitive personality and that driven, high-achieving attitude can cause a real crash if you push yourself too far.

Anna Hemmings MBE is probably Britain's most successful ever female canoeist, a two-time Olympian and six-time world champion. However, after 15 years at the highest level of the sport, she crashed. Her body gave up and said, "No more."

The singer Cher developed the same thing. As did Flea, the bass player from the Red Hot Chili Peppers.

Be aware that although it's good to be busy, it's also very good to take time out.

EXERCISE

WHAT DO YOU LOVE TO DO?

It's time to grab your pen and paper, sit down somewhere and write out a list of things you really love doing.

- Ask yourself: what are the activities that you enjoy more than anything?

- List as many as you can, no matter how simple or how pointless they may seem.

- Plan when to do them.

- Put it in your diary to remind you that it's important.

- Be realistic. Schedule in steps that lead you to the activity if needs be, not just the activity itself. If it's a day off work to play seven hours of video games that you want, then schedule time into your diary to speak to your boss about the best time to do it. You might just find that your boss doesn't care which day you take off because the company isn't actually going to fall apart without you after all.

But, I Want To Be Perfect

I'd been working as a therapist for about five years and had recently got married when I started to get a bit too busy. As well as my job, I was working on the committee of a hypnotherapy members' organisation and was also on the committee of a theatre company too, and so I didn't have a great deal of spare time to do paperwork. Even a therapist has paperwork you know – it's not all sitting down and saying, "How does that make you feel?" for hours on end. So I took the brave and noble decision not to see clients on Fridays.

Taking a day off work might not sound very brave or noble, but it meant I had to stop working from one particular location that I enjoyed, so I was determined to make the best use of this day off.

So, on my way to the pub one Friday afternoon to meet my wife on her lunch break, she called me to let me know that her and her workmates were running a few minutes late. She asked if I could get everyone some drinks. Four women, four Diet Cokes. "OK," I said, and so I did.

It was a typical Friday lunchtime queue in the pub and the ladies were very grateful that they didn't have to wait; they could just walk in, sit down and begin their girly chats. It felt good to be of service; I didn't really know these friends of my wife very well and I wanted to make a good impression.

It was probably 30 seconds before one of them began talking about their frustrations with their boyfriend, and another 30 seconds before someone else joined in with theirs, and this went on for an hour. My wife was unable to join in because I was sitting right next to her. It was at this point that I realised I shouldn't really be wasting my paperwork day in the pub, and that I might not actually be that welcome anyway. I was one of the enemy, after all.

Now, I hear these sorts of stories in my consulting room all the time; women regularly talk about how their partner has upset them and blame them for their anxiety and depression. But in my whole life, I'd never actually gone out for a drink with nothing but a group of women to hear those same stories without being paid for it.

It made me wonder what my wife would have said had I not been there. Would she have complained that I was untidy, that I don't pull my weight with housework? Would she have said that I was inattentive and not considerate to her needs?

I went home to do paperwork, but ended up putting the vacuum cleaner around the house and made sure all the toilet seats were down.

I thought of myself as a great husband, but what if I wasn't? The idea that my wife would sit and slag me off every Friday afternoon with her friends over Diet Cokes and crisps was more than just daunting; it actually touched a raw nerve that I didn't even realise was there. I wanted to be perfect.

I wanted my wife to sit around that table and think to herself. "Holy crap, I'm so glad I married the man I did; everyone else's seems to be awful. There's no way I'm letting him go."

And so I did my best to be the perfect husband. I'd give a foot massage twice per week, a back massage every night in bed. I'd wake her up every morning with a little kiss and get her a glass of water. I let her make the decisions over what we'd eat for our evening meals and I'd ask her what SHE wanted to do rather than tell her what I wanted, because I could be happy with anything but she might have a preference. It never really occurred to me that I might resent this, and it certainly never occurred to me that SHE might resent it.

But after years and years of this, what started off as me just wanting to be the perfect husband means that I now have a wife who's fed up with having to make all the decisions. And in the build-up to her 40th birthday, she's getting very annoyed that I'm almost constantly asking her what she wants, because she keeps telling me that she doesn't want anything. She's not materialistic and doesn't like getting stuff just for the sake of it.

But, I want to be the perfect husband. I want her to sit around with her friends and when they ask, "What did Rich get you for your birthday?" she can flash some gorgeous piece of jewellery or pull out some new car keys. Nope, that's not going to happen, because every time I bring up the idea of going shopping for her to choose something for her 40th, she reiterates that she doesn't want anything; she bought a new car the previous year and loves it, she has enough jewellery as it is that she doesn't wear and I'm not to waste my money on more, so let's go away somewhere instead. "Let's have a city break," she says. Sounds great to me – that way I can take her shopping so that she's got something tangible for her birthday.

So, we go to Edinburgh for a few days and try to catch a glimpse of some pandas in the zoo, we admire the architecture, the history and we have a great time, except that I keep trying to drag her into every department store we walk past to get her a birthday present. "I didn't come here to go shopping, I can do that at home!" is the constant response. This is when my anxiety really starts to kick in; it's been there in the background for a few weeks, but now I'm beginning to panic.

We get back home the night before her birthday and I haven't bought her anything. All she has is a card with some soppy comments and smudged biro drawings of love hearts and kisses.

But I want to be the perfect husband! Well, how's that working out for you, Rich? In my quest to be perfect, I've created a marriage where my wife makes all the decisions, where I'm scared to make my own in case they're wrong and it looks like I could have ruined her 40th birthday. But maybe I'm worrying for no reason. After all, she constantly said that she didn't want anything for her birthday and that's what she's got, so maybe she'll laugh about it.

She didn't talk to me for two weeks.

What I learned from that experience is that being the ideal husband isn't about being perfect. If I want my wife to think to herself that there's nothing she'd change about me, then that's not because I have no flaws. It's because any flaws that I do have are easily overlooked because she respects me. And I'm pretty sure that had it not come to a head because of her birthday, that respect would not have lasted very much longer.

CHECKING FOR DOUBLE STANDARDS

This exercise will help you to recognise if there are any expectations you have for yourself that have been set too high.

EXERCISE

- Grab a pen and some paper and sit down for 15 minutes.

- Have a think about the standards that you set yourself in one particular area of your life, whether that's in your relationship, at work, as a friend or as a parent.

- Pick one area to work on and write a list of your expectations. Maybe you want to be the employee that always leaves their desk empty at the end of the day or the dad who never loses his temper.

- List as many behaviours or traits that you expect of yourself as you can.

- Go through the list again, only this time see those standards as someone else's – someone that you are close to and have great respect for. Pick a close friend or family member and cross off any expectations that you think it would be unfair for you to have of them.

EXERCISE

- Now ask yourself what effect crossing off those expectations would have if you applied them to yourself. Does the world still spin? Does everything work out OK despite it?

- Do the same for other areas of your life. Come back to it another day if you need to.

- Make a new list of all the expectations you crossed off from the different areas of your life.

- Pick one that you crossed off and think about how you would act differently in life if you no longer had this expectation and deliberately integrate it into your day. Maybe you create an expectation that you'll send an email without rewriting it twice first or deliberately leave the vacuuming for 24 hours after you first feel the need to do it.

- When you feel ready, the following day, the following week or maybe further ahead if you need to, look through your list again and pick another one to integrate into your life.

Resilience

Let me tell you about a psychology teacher named Jessica Hartnett.

In the autumn of 2007, at Northern Illinois University, Jessica started research into what's called affective forecasting.[37] This is about predicting how we will feel in the future about something that has just happened.

Previous studies have shown that we tend to overestimate the influence of both positive and negative events.

Using what is called the Profile of Mood States (POMS), students who took part were simply ticking boxes on a computer program that asked them to rate how highly they felt a variety of emotions.

All started out fine until Valentine's Day 2008 when one of the students at the university took four guns into school and shot 26 people, five of whom died, and then he killed himself.

The school was closed for a week and, after a memorial, it was opened back up so that everyone could try to put their lives back together as best they could.

Jessica's research carried on for another two weeks, but because there had been an obvious change in everyone's circumstances, the original study had to be scrapped.

The one useful by-product of this terrible tragedy was that it allowed Jessica to compare how people felt before and then after a serious psychological trauma.

What she discovered is that, despite what had happened to them, everyone was surprisingly positive.

Let me tell you a little about the Profile of Mood States.

It goes through a 36-item scale that asks participants to

rate, from 1 to 5, the extent to which they are currently experiencing a variety of different emotions that can be split into 6 subscales:

Depression
Vigour
Tension
Fatigue
Confusion
Anger

Here's what she found:

	Before Shooting:	After Shooting:
Depression:	1.48	1.52
Vigour:	2.20	2.11
Tension:	1.51	1.51
Fatigue:	2.12	2.17
Confusion:	1.68	1.79
Anger:	1.43	1.70

The only slight shift is anger, and then it wasn't even by half a point.

Now, here's the really interesting part.

The following year, they repeated the exercise with new students but asked the participants to fill it in twice. The second time they were asked to fill it in based on how they imagined they would feel if they had been a student at the time of the shooting.

What it showed is that they massively underestimated

how emotionally strong they are likely to have been. The table below compares the participants' responses from the previous year after the shooting with the participants from the following year imagining how they would have responded.

	After Real Shooting:	After Imagined Shooting:
Depression:	1.52	3.00
Vigour:	2.11	1.95
Tension:	1.51	3.43
Fatigue:	2.17	3.07
Confusion:	1.79	2.85
Anger:	1.70	3.28

Their expectation of depression and anger was almost double the scores of the real students. Tension was predicted at even more than double and their expectation of vigour and fatigue was totally wrong too.

It seems we are not very good at predicting to what degree negative events would upset us.

In fact, if you look at student attendance at that same university, in the year of the shooting virtually no students dropped out of their course. Yet it's typical for a university to routinely lose 15% of its students in a year.

It appears that something at that university encouraged students to complete their studies, when they wouldn't normally have done so.

It seems that Friedrich Nietzsche was right with his famous quote, "That which does not kill us makes us stronger." Knowing that this quote is actually more than just a cliché can allow us to let go of our fears of the future.

It turns out that it won't actually matter if we make the wrong decision with our degree, our job or our relationship. We will get over a bad situation quite quickly and become more resilient because of it.

Married With Children

All of my one-to-one clients fill in an intake form prior to starting personal therapy with me. It asks for hobbies and interests, their job, their medical history and also asks their marital status and how many children they have. It's useful for me to know because it gives us something to talk about if the client isn't quite sure why they're there; occasionally clients will come to me saying that they don't know quite what's wrong but they know they aren't feeling right. So seeing whether they are single at 30 or childless at 45 makes for some interesting conversation openers.

In our modern society there seems to be a social stigma attached to being single, particularly so for women in their late 20s and mid-30s according to a study by Elizabeth Sharp, Professor of Human Development and Family Studies at Texas Tech University.[38] So when I see on an intake form that my client is the wrong side of 35, has no children or is unmarried, or both, I'll enquire about how they feel about relationships and children. Most people seem to think it's important to them, a handful of folk don't care either way, and a small minority of them are genuinely not interested in marriage or children. But more of them think that it's important than don't.

Yet, if you ask people if they think that being single means it's impossible to be happy, most of them will say no. I know that's what they say because I've asked them. When pressed to explain why they think that way, they come up with all these reasons why single people can still be happy without a partner. Then you ask them if they are married themselves. If you then ask, "Do you want to be married?" almost all of the currently married folk will say yes and just as many of the single ones will too.

It seems that even though we intellectually think that being single won't affect our long-term happiness, there is a foundation to our belief system that pulls us towards marriage anyway. But what's the truth? If we're single, should we prioritise a relationship or should we embrace single life and see if we can live happily ever after on our own? What do all the studies prove?

Unfortunately, no one can make up their mind about what the studies prove, which tells me that it doesn't really matter either way. Proponents of the "marriage makes you happy" brigade will often cite the same research[39] as the "marriage makes no difference" brigade. Both groups interpret the findings in their own way to prove their existing beliefs.[40] The problem here is divorce. If you take couples who divorce out of the equation altogether, as a lot of analysts do, then you're only left with a pot of mostly happily married people to compare to the single folk. If this was a study investigating how effective medication is on wellbeing, we wouldn't be able to delete the people that gave up on it because it was making them ill. The same should apply with marriage research.

It is true that there is a correlation between marriage and happiness, but it's not fully understood which one is influencing which. Are happy people more likely to get married or is it that getting married makes you happier? We don't know. As a scientist, if you really wanted to figure it out, you have to use the gold standard method, which would mean you'd have to randomly assign people to either get married or stay single, then assign the married group to more groups instructing them to get divorced or widowed. You would monitor them all over the course of ten years or so and see what happens. Not surprisingly, no university seems willing to take the idea on board yet.

The only type of study you can do instead, is one where you simply monitor a load of random people with questionnaires and see how they all cope with various life experiences. Stick all the data into a computer and try as best you can to match up groups of people who all have similar experiences and then see if their happiness levels change if you add getting married into the equation. It's not an easy task, but a few people have done it. In their 2012 study 'Does Personality Moderate Reaction and Adaptation to Major Life Events?' Stevie Yap, Ivana Anusic and Richard Lucas of Michigan State University (MSU), analysed the British Household Panel Survey and published their findings in the *Journal of Research in Personality*. It must have been painstaking work and I applaud them for their diligence. But whether I forgive them for classing participants as single when they got divorced or their partner died, is another question.

In a major analysis of previous studies, Richard Lucas of MSU, this time with Andrew Clark of the Paris School of Economics, produced their paper 'Do People Really Adapt To Marriage?' As well as re-examining the 10,000 individuals in the British Household Panel Survey, they also pored over the German Socio-Economic Panel Study data from an 18-year study of more than 30,000 Germans. Then they took a deep breath and turned to The 2002 World Values Survey, a huge database put together by a global network of social scientists studying changing values and their impact on social and political life.

Each of the married people in the studies was matched up with a single person of a similar age, sex, education and income. Their overall happiness was measured on a seven-point scale, revealing that the people who got married and stayed married were happier, but just under a third of one point (0.28 to be precise), than those that had stayed single.

At the point of getting married, the difference was a little higher, with 0.48 more happiness than their single counterparts, dropping gradually every year following the wedding until the difference was only 0.28.

In short, what they all seem to show is that right before the wedding there is a nice increase in wellbeing that peaks right afterwards, lasts for a year or so before starting to gently drop down year after year until somewhere between six and ten years later it's pretty much the same as it was beforehand. So, if someone was unhappy before the wedding, they become unhappy again later on. If they were happy beforehand, then they get a little happier for a while and then might as well not have bothered. So, yes marriage can make you a little happier, even if only for a short while. But then, so can getting divorced.

These same studies also show that getting divorced can make you just as happy as getting married does. Does this mean that we have to keep getting married and then divorced as many times as we can? Accumulating more and more happiness every time? No, of course not. What the research shows is that happy marriages can make you happy and getting out of a miserable marriage also makes you happy.

So if someone was to make a list of things to do to increase happiness, getting married wouldn't be on the list. The differences have been proven to be so statistically insignificant that it just isn't worth doing. But obviously there are plenty of other reasons to get married. I'm certainly not saying NEVER get married. What I'm saying is don't get married thinking that it will make you happier, because it won't.

If you spent the early part of your life dreaming of settling down with the perfect partner so as to make the perfect life then you made a mistake. It's not your fault, you were probably brainwashed by a society that encourages marriage and you had no reason to doubt it. I don't blame you. I used to believe that carrots made you see in the dark, until I found out it was a myth popularised by a World War II propaganda campaign. I used to believe in Father Christmas and the Tooth Fairy until I was old enough to think for myself. For a brief period when I was seven I thought the only way to be happy was to have a Big Trak toy and a copy of the *Beano*.

If you are single and miserable, with a belief that you can only be happy in life if you settle down and get married, then you've been poorly informed, and it is that belief that is preventing you from enjoying being single.

I know that this research might sound counter-intuitive, but it gets worse. A lot of people don't like to agree with these studies because of the effects that having children seems to have on happiness levels. Almost everyone I talk to about this says that they are the exception to the rule, myself included. But the results of multiple studies, including the empirical work based on data from the first 20 years of the

West German sub-sample of the German Socio-Economic Panel, and published by the Institute for the Study of Labor (IZA) in 2006, show us that having children does not actually make us any happier.

I know that those of you who have children will say that it doesn't apply to you, and I get it. When I read through the IZA research paper that raised awareness of this anomaly, I said that it didn't apply to me too, because my son is the greatest source of happiness I have in my life. Yet studies throughout English-speaking nations consistently show that people without children are happier than people with children.[41]

In 2003, Jean Twenge of San Diego State University, W. Keith Campbell from the University of Georgia and Craig A. Foster of the US Air Force Academy published their findings in *The Journal of Marriage and Family*. Titled 'Parenthood and Marital Satisfaction: A Meta-Analytic Review', the findings suggested that the reason having children doesn't increase happiness could be because of marital dissatisfaction due to role conflicts and restrictions of freedom.

These studies led Jennifer Glass of the University of Texas, Robin W. Simon from Wake Forest University and Matthew A. Andersson of the University of Iowa to look at a data set from not just English-speaking countries but also from further afield. In their snappily titled 2016 paper 'Parenthood and Happiness: Effects of Work-Family Reconciliation Policies in 22 OECD Countries', they suggest that the negative effect that having children has on our wellbeing can be explained by the absence of social policies that allow parents to better combine work with family life.

Their findings show that some countries (Portugal, Hungary and Spain) actually have a significant positive response to having children, possibly due to extended family being able to offer support. Portuguese parents had an 8% increase in wellbeing, Hungarians a 4.7% boost and Spain a 3.1% improvement. By contrast, the United States showed a 12% decrease, Ireland a 9.5% drop and Britain an 8% reduction in happiness.

It's worth mentioning, though, that this study was done country by country, so parents in Portugal were compared with non-parents in Portugal, for example, to look for differences. Portugal, Hungary and Spain might have scored quite highly in happiness effects from having children but they are still quite low in happiness levels overall compared to the UK and US. According to the World Happiness Report, in which you may remember that Norway is number 1 and Central African Republic is 155, Portugal ranks 89, Hungary 75 and Spain 34.

Comparing happiness from around the world can be tricky, because concepts of happiness tend to differ among cultures. But what we see is that having a child and then trying to carry on with life as before actually seems to have a significant negative effect on our wellbeing. Yet very few parents will believe it. In the same way that if you'd have told me aged seven that I didn't need a Big Trak and the *Beano* to be happy I wouldn't have believed you, because it was all I wanted. It seems that it's the same when it comes to having children; they might be what we want, but not what we need.

So why does pretty much every parent say the opposite to the researchers' findings? Why does every parent say that they are happier because they have a child? It's simply because they don't have access to the universe where they didn't have a child to know how they feel in it. The question:

"Would you be less or more happy if you had never had your child?" gets interpreted as "Would you be less or more happy if you lost your child?", to which there's only one sensible answer.

Also, there's the phenomenon of cognitive dissonance, a state of mental conflict that comes from holding two opposing opinions at the same time. The mind doesn't like this and so seeks to resolve it by having you change your beliefs or change your behaviour in some way.

The psychologist Leon Festinger was one of the first to publish findings that showed that this phenomenon exists[42] when he proved that he could influence how much people were happy to perform a boring task by giving them money.

The task was to use one hand to pick up spools of thread and put them onto trays before emptying them and then starting again. After they'd done that for half an hour, they then had to use the same hand to turn the spools one at a time by a quarter of a turn until they were all back to their original positions. It was dull and repetitive and was designed in such a way as to be as boring as they could make it. Some were given no money at all, some were given $1, and some got $20. You'd think that those who were paid the most cash would be the ones who claimed to enjoy it the most wouldn't you? Nope. Rather than feel they wasted their time, the participants that only received $1 claimed to actually enjoy it a little bit. By contrast, those that either received no money at all or got $20 hated every second. This is called the 'overjustification hypothesis', in which our brain plays tricks on us. We make things up and lie to ourselves without even realising it. If we do something with very little or no reward, we seem to warrant doing it by telling ourselves it must have been worth it in other ways. Yet when rewarded for it, our only reason for doing it was to get the reward, therefore we didn't enjoy it.

This is the mistake we make in thinking that getting a pay rise will make our job better; this experiment suggests that we will actually enjoy our job less the more that we're paid.

It's the reason why the iPhone is as popular as it is, despite the fact that it's way more expensive than it should be. If it was cheaper, people wouldn't value it so highly and it would become less desirable. I remember buying one when they first came out; they were a luxury item with a contract that cost more per month than I paid in electricity for my whole house. But wow, look at it! You can watch *Doctor Who* on it, you can find the nearest Starbucks on it, my calendar and emails are on here so I never need to carry a Filofax again. "Yes Richard, but couldn't you do that with your old phone?" Shut up conscience, go back to sleep. This phone is totally worth it, and I'm going to tell everyone that they should get one too.

It seems that having children is a bit like that. We value them because of the cost they come with. It's a huge sacrifice to your quality of sleep, your bank balance and your social functioning. Having children is a hard, thankless task and if we didn't offset it with a belief that it was the right thing to do, we'd bang our heads against the wall every day screaming "What have I done?" Of course, I'm the exception to the rule here and if you have kids then I bet that you are too. Because all of the love and the pride I experience because I have a son far outweighs the worry, the drop in self-importance and the loss of hair. I am very happy with my family life and wouldn't change it for anything. But am I happy BECAUSE I am a parent or am I happy DESPITE being a parent?

It's an uncomfortable question that no parent wants to think about, and so we leave it to the academics to figure out for us. But, because the answers keep coming up as negative, scholars are constantly going back through data searching for a way to disprove the correlation. Contrary to popular belief, the scientific method is about trying to prove your theories wrong, not prove them right.

Using data sets from all over the world, from surveys that asked a similarly phrased question as "Taking all things together, how would you say things are with you – would you say you're very happy, fairly happy, or not too happy these days?", the outcomes from the British Household Panel Survey, the German Socio-Economic Panel Study, the 2002 World Values Survey, the Euro-Barometer Survey Series and the United States General Social Survey all give us evidence that, on average, parents report statistically significantly lower levels of happiness than non-parents. They show that there is a slight increase in wellbeing shortly before the time of the birth for women, but not for men. Then immediately following the birth of the child, wellbeing for both of them begins to decline steadily for around four years showing quite significant unhappiness before returning to the same level that it was had they not bothered having children in the first place.

So, if you've made the decision not to have children and you think you might be missing out on a chunk of happiness, you're not. If you're panicking that you're running out of time to find Mr or Mrs Right and start a family, then chill out. If you do, you'll be happy, but if you don't, you'll still be happy. Remember that being a parent is a choice, not an obligation.

EXERCISE

SETTING STANDARDS

If you're worried that lowering your standards will mean you'll let yourself slip and become careless, here are some things to remember to help you to address your fears.

- If you have mixed feelings about the idea of lowering your standards in an area of your life, it can be a good idea to make a list of pros and cons. What are the positives in keeping these standards? What benefits does it give you? What are the costs that come with holding on to these standards? What negative effect is it having on other areas of your life?

- Recognise that in lowering your standards it doesn't mean that you'll have no standards at all. Realistic standards can actually help you to do your best without damaging your mental health and getting in the way of things that are important to you.

- Remember that it's OK to ask for help. It might be hard to know how to lower an unrealistic standard to a more reasonable level. Ask a friend or someone that you trust who does not have problems with perfectionism to help you with setting new realistic standards. What do they do that works? It can help you realise just how unreasonable you may have been to yourself.

It's OK To Be A Loser

I saw a post on social media recently with a quote from Ted Turner, the founder of CNN and the guy who donated $1 billion to the United Nations. It said: "You can never quit. Winners never quit, and quitters never win." It was followed up by another one, this time by Zig Ziglar, the author of dozens of personal development books (who despite dying in 2012 still seems to be a prolific Twitter user), who said, "You were born to win, but to be a winner, you must plan to win, prepare to win, and expect to win."

I was unsure whether these two posts were saying similar things or opposing things. And I didn't know whether I agreed with either of them or not. Thinking of yourself as a winner sounds like a positive attitude that sets you up for a happy and successful life, but maybe it's a bit of a con. I'm not saying that thinking of yourself as a loser is such a good idea either though, but maybe there's a middle ground.

Winning can make you complacent; it's how con artists manage to trick people on holiday into parting with their money with the Three-Card Monte trick. If you've never seen this it's where three cards are shown face up and then rearranged face down. Your job is to find the money card, often the queen of hearts, and if you find it you win. The con artist will sometimes let someone win a few times to get their confidence up before fleecing them of everything in their wallet. Their confidence was high because they had no experience of losing, but it was false confidence.

When my son was younger I often tricked him in a similar, but less financially crushing way. If you have children, then I'm sure you understand that if they were to lose at every single game of noughts and crosses for an entire afternoon, then very soon something is going to get thrown at the wall. Every now and again, you let them win for the sake of the wallpaper. But that process can come at a cost.

A few years ago I was teaching my son how to play draughts (or checkers, depending on which century or country you live in) and applied the same principle. He wasn't going to enjoy losing every time and that lack of enjoyment would get in the way of him learning. So I sometimes made some deliberate mistakes that he took advantage of, and humbly accepted that he beat me. It's quite a lengthy game, so we probably only played it once or twice per day. But I noticed that every time he won he would play the next game too quickly, even if it was the following day. He wouldn't think ahead and the game would be over in half the time with me the victor. Then the game after that would be a bit slower, he'd concentrate, think ahead and then beat me fairly and squarely. He became a winner only because he had previously been a loser.

I think that we need to be comfortable with being the loser from time to time. But recent culture seems to be obsessed with winning, with being the best. As I'm writing this it's August, the month where students throughout the UK get their A-Level and GCSE results. All across the news, all over social media and all through Chicken Cottage and McDonalds, we're hearing that everyone wants to be an A-star student. News crews are on their way to the selected school, ready to capture a student's face as they rip open their envelope to find that (surprise, surprise) the student that the school suggested the news crew interview only went and did really well!

And the students that 'only' received Bs and Cs will have

to watch this on TV that evening, over an evening meal that they can't eat because they're sick to their stomach, berating themselves for their inadequate result while they contemplate a life without a degree and a future without a career. At what point did getting below an A-grade become failing? When did going to a university become an indicator of a happier future than one with an apprenticeship, anyway? If it's because of the idea of earning more money as a university graduate then I'm afraid we've already highlighted in an earlier chapter that money isn't that important, not that a graduate will earn more anyway.

According to findings by the Sutton Trust in their 2015 report 'The Potential of UK Apprenticeships',[43] the only UK graduates that do have a greater earning potential are the ones from the top Russell Group universities like Oxford and Cambridge, and even then it's not much more than someone who studies for a Level 5 apprenticeship level with just three C-grade A-levels. The same report even found that, because of tuition fees, a graduate qualifying from most universities could actually be worse off, so it's definitely not about the money. It's about feeling proud of ourselves, and there's so much more in life to be proud about than our qualifications. So, if you have a chip on your shoulder about not going to university or are still beating yourself up because you didn't finish high school, then you need to give yourself a break. The fact that you had enough ambition to desire it is what counts, not whether you were able to or not.

It reminds me of when I was Development Director at the National Council for Hypnotherapy. One of my responsibilities was to get in touch with some randomly chosen therapists throughout the country and ask them to confirm what Continuing Professional Development (CPD) they had undertaken in the previous 12 months. In order to remain registered, we expected members to have at least read a few journals over the course of a year, if not attended some weekend course somewhere. When enquiring what these therapists had been up to with their CPD, they seemed to fall into one of three categories:

1. These are the courses I attended and some books I read; it's more than you wanted. Let's all live happily ever after.

2. I'm so sorry, I would have loved to have done something, but just wasn't able to for lots of silly reasons. All I did was read journals and books and articles on the internet. I will do better this year, I swear.

3. I haven't done anything and I'm offended that you asked me. I've been a therapist for 20 years and there's nothing I don't already know. Be gone with you.

Ideally, everyone would be in the first category. But of the other two, which one should be most proud of themselves – the one that beats themselves up because they wanted to do something but didn't? Or the one that thinks they know everything and doesn't need to develop themselves? I know which one I'd prefer to be my therapist. The world is constantly changing, especially in the field of mental health, and a therapist who thinks they already know everything and doesn't need to learn anything new is going to fall behind and become the exact opposite to the know-it-all they think they are.

The same goes for development at any age, especially education. Which child has the better foundations for success – the one that goes to an Ofsted Outstanding-rated school but doesn't want to learn? Or the kid who goes to an Inadequate-rated school, but has an enthusiasm for learning? The desire to want to do well is going to have a massive bearing. Yet so many parents will stress over making sure that their child goes to the best school that they can find, not realising that all their children probably need is for their parents to be a good inspiration to them. Wanting your children to do well is going to be good enough to set them up nicely for life. Even if they do fail along the way, even if they aren't top of the class. It's OK to be average.

When Michael Gove was the UK Secretary of State for Education a few years ago, he said that every student should exceed the national average.

Now, I got a D in my GCSE maths exam (twice) and dropped out of college because of it, but even I know that everyone being above average is mathematically impossible. If being average isn't good enough for a modern society then everyone's self-esteem is going to drop and there's going to be an even greater increase in what's called imposter syndrome.

Impostor syndrome is a concept that describes people who are marked by an inability to recognise their accomplishments. It can cause those who reach a moderate level of success to develop a persistent fear of being exposed as an imposter or a fraud. The term was coined in 1978 by clinical psychologists Pauline R. Clance and Suzanne A. Imes, who observed that despite external evidence of their competence, people exhibiting the syndrome remained convinced, that they did not deserve the success they had achieved. When shown proof of their success, it was dismissed as luck, timing, or as a result of deceiving others into thinking they were more intelligent and competent than they believed themselves to be.

Clance and Imes' research from the early 1980s estimated that two out of five successful people consider themselves frauds. More recently, in 2011, psychologists Jaruwan Sakulku and James Alexander performed a meta-analysis on articles about the factors that contribute to imposter syndrome.[44] They found that 70% of all people feel like impostors at one time or another. So, if you've ever thought to yourself, "One of these days everyone will find out that I'm not as clever as they think I am," then you're in good company because there's hardly a successful person in the world who doesn't at some point have self-doubt, a doubt that feeds a belief that you're actually nobody special and that any achievements you've had were down to luck rather than ability.

The reason for this is because of what is often called the Dunning-Kruger effect, so called after David Dunning and Justin Kruger of Cornell University, who conducted some experiments[45] in the field of cognitive bias during the late 1990s. They had previously observed that we actually find it quite hard to notice when we are performing at our best. There is usually a big difference with being the best version of ourselves and being the best in the world. And because we tend to look at others to compare our achievements, and often with those who ARE the best in the world, we can easily overlook our own achievements.

It does often work the opposite way around though too,

where people can sometimes think they're more talented than they actually are. The conclusion that Dunning and Kruger came to sounds quite obvious when you think about it, that if you are actually incompetent, you can't know that you are incompetent. In their research, they stumbled across a lot of people who were too stupid to know just how stupid they actually were. As William Shakespeare said in *As You Like It*, "The fool doth think he is wise, but the wise man knows himself to be a fool."

For a while, the Dunning-Kruger effect was called the *American Idol* effect, and if you've ever watched things like *The X Factor*, you'll know why. So often you will listen to someone singing atrociously, who afterwards will stand, smiling, in front of the audience and judges saying, "Ain't I amazing!" while everyone takes their fingers back out of their ears.

They genuinely cannot tell that they are dreadful singers because they are tone deaf; to them their singing voice sounds the same as a professional's voice does, in the same way that I cannot tell the difference between a painting by Leonardo da Vinci and one by Michelangelo because I don't know what I'm looking for.

But this process has the reverse effect too. Immediately following the painful performance of the dreadful singer is someone with the most beautiful voice who can't recognise how good they are. Once their musical ability to hear notes improves and they can notice the difference between a high C at 262hz and a C# at 277hz they can pick up on their own faults, especially if they constantly compare themselves to the best singers in the world.

These characters will perform to the judges and even make

them cry but they almost always get told the same thing: "Your confidence lets you down; your belief in yourself is holding you back." That's imposter syndrome at work there.

Even Albert Einstein suffered from it, although not with singing, as far as I know. A month before he died, he confided to Queen Elisabeth of Belgium and said, "The exaggerated esteem in which my lifework is held makes me very ill at ease. I feel compelled to think of myself as an involuntary swindler."

Too often we fall into the trap of comparing our weaknesses with other people's strengths. We say to ourselves, "If only I could speak as confidently as Jeff," or "If only I was as clever as Joan." Meanwhile, all the Jeffs and Joans are thinking, "If only I was as creative or as funny as you."

When comparing our insides with other people's outsides, all we get is our imagination creating a perception of a reality that doesn't even exist.

Thinking this way is totally human, and it's something we all do. So it is important to be aware of it in order to prevent it from turning into negative thinking that harms our self-esteem.

Remember that bravery doesn't mean feeling confident, it means feeling nervous but doing something anyway. And we need bravery to take risks, to take on challenges and pursue ideas that leave us open to the possibility of failing and of being "found out". In simply attempting to accomplish something, whether you actually manage it or not, you will still achieve more than if you'd not tried in the first place.

Psychological research like the studies by Dunning and Kruger, and Sakulku and Alexander shows us that almost all successful people will consider themselves to be a fraud at some point in their lives, so it's obviously quite normal. It's how we deal with it that influences our belief about ourselves. If we embrace it as truth then it will get us down. But if we can recognise that it's just a trick of the mind, it's easier to challenge that inner critic.

What's interesting is that those people who set the bar quite low in life don't tend to suffer with imposter syndrome; it's those that work hard and diligently that do. Furthermore, the harder we work the more praise we end up getting from people, which increases our success and makes us more likely to move up in the world. As we move up, it's likely we'll be exposed to more and more of the things we don't know, maintaining these fears of being found out to be a fraud.

But it's all just our internal perception. If we only ever compare ourselves to someone that we perceive is amazing, then we're only going to feel rubbish about ourselves. There's nothing wrong with having a positive opinion of someone, but it shouldn't be at the expense of our self-esteem. I wonder how many artists, songwriters or authors are put off because they compare themselves to the best in the world and don't even get off the starting blocks of their careers because of their fears. Yet, if we have some patience and diligence, we can be anything we want to be; it just takes enthusiasm and hard work.

The best songwriters and authors do not want to be reminded of their early works; the Brontë sisters may have written some of the most praised works in English literature but if you read their early stories, they're dreadful. If they knew it, it didn't stop them because they wrote hundreds of stories, getting better as they practised. Even David Bowie found it hard to listen to one of his very early singles. 'The

Laughing Gnome' was a song he was never allowed to forget because his record company re-released it after he became well known, much to his annoyance. Making a joke of it, he wrote a sequel for Comic Relief in 1999. He called it 'Requiem for a Laughing Gnome', which was a four-hour song for solo recorder, with viewers invited to donate money to get him to stop playing it.

Bowie and the Brontë sisters were not born with abilities or skills to be able to write words that would be so lauded in the future; they needed to practise as they learned. But, whether we're learning to be an author or learning how to be happier, everything takes practice and comparing ourselves to people that already can do those things can either inspire us to practise or prevent us from even getting started, depending on the way we look at it.

Those TV shows like *The X Factor* and *Britain's Got Talent* are a great platform that give opportunities to people that probably wouldn't get the chance to prove themselves to an audience. They're not just a bit of fun; sometimes these competitions are life-changing. They're about giving people the chance to give up their day job. *The X Factor* offers the winners a recording contract! It changes their lives. But not just the lives of the winners. Many of the runners-up have gone on to have enormous success, in many cases greater than those who beat them in the final. If One Direction, Olly Murs and Susan Boyle had thought of themselves as losers for not winning and had walked away from music it would have been a great shame. Yet so often you hear contestants who get through to the live shows say things like, "If I don't win, I'm never singing again. This was my only chance." And if they don't win, they feel like a failure and walk away from their dreams forever. Not being the best in the world at something does not make you a failure!

Getting a 2:2 or a third-class honours degree is not failing at getting a degree. And similarly, I'm sorry to all you successful first-class honours achievers out there, but you're no more successful at life than anyone else, unless getting that degree was your ONLY goal in life, which you might think it is, but usually there's a reason for the degree. It's worth looking at what's underneath our goals to work out what we really want.

It could be that your only goal in life is to be happy and, in doing so, you will succeed in your goal, but if you do all the wrong things thinking that it eventually leads to happiness then you might be disappointed. There's a phrase I use a lot in my therapy room: "There's nothing worse than spending your whole life climbing a ladder only to get to the top and find you had it leant against the wrong wall."

Some of the happiest people you meet won't necessarily be people that modern society would class as successful. There's a strong chance that they don't have a degree. The UK Census of 2011 showed that only 27% of adults were educated to degree level and almost 23% had no qualifications at all. Being successful is very subjective; it means something different to everyone and so it can't really be measured. How can you tell if a school is a success? Well, you set targets and see how many pupils reach them. But those targets are set externally. They have to be, because if you set your own targets then you can deliberately set them low in order to achieve them, and if we lived that way then one person's success would be another one's failure. Well, yeah, that's life actually, and we all need to be aware of it. We need to understand that sometimes achievements that are reached by hitting targets that were set by other people mean nothing – it's just a game that we have to play sometimes.

Because of this, it's OK to set your own targets and be happy. Is someone who lives in the same rented house for ten years less of a success than the one who lives in their own home, which they still owe the bank 50 grand for? I'd say no. But if getting out of renting is the only thing that you think will make you happy, then finally getting a mortgage and moving house will cheer you up for a little while, probably about a year if research into habituation is anything to go by. Professor Sonja Lyubomirsky has devoted many years to the study of habituation and the way we adapt to change, and finds that 12 months is about the norm before your levels of happiness go right back to what they were before you bought it. This is only going to be OK if you were already happy in the first place and the new house is the icing on the cake. If you weren't happy in the first place, because living in the rented house meant you hadn't hit your target, then you didn't know how to be happy. You'd set your target not just too high but in the wrong area completely, and the bloke next door who carries on renting but still whistles everywhere he goes with a smile on his face and pride in his heart certainly doesn't need to be looked down on because he doesn't own his own home, does he?

In life we can set our own targets, our own goals. And just because your fitness instructor says you should have done a five-mile run, but you only did three miles, did you fail? In their eyes maybe, but not in yours, especially if your goal was just to get off your backside and do something. Anything is still better than nothing.

I'll never forget the furious look on a friend of mine's face when she and her sister went to a slimming group and, although she'd lost three pounds in a week, her sister had lost twice as much, and the consultant running the group said to my friend, "What did you do wrong?" She'd done nothing wrong – losing three pounds is fine, more than fine actually. But I tell you what she did right: she didn't go back, that's what she did. What would the instructor have said if she hadn't lost any weight at all yet? When clients come to me for help with weight loss, I don't really want to see much change in the first week, because it's not sustainable and can set them up for feeling like a failure.

Failing is part of the process of learning, and we all have to be OK with it. We're all going to fail more often than we succeed. How many job interviews do we have to go to before we get one job: five, ten? How many CVs do we have to send out before we even get a call for the interview in the first place: 50? 100?

If you see every ignored job application as a failure, rather than simply part of the job-seeking process, then you're going to become very disillusioned with life. Making mistakes and experiencing setbacks are a normal and recurrent part of life. As the old Chinese proverb says, "Fall down seven times and get up eight." Which is exactly how toddlers learn to walk. As adults we need to have the same attitude: to accept failure and mistakes as part of the learning process and move on from them. Little children learning to walk don't have the critical voice in their head saying, "You can't do this, you're crap" like us adults do, so they don't give up. They see adults walking around them and copy them until they get it right.

In the absence of any serious disability they never accept they can't do something. In fact there are plenty of youngsters with a disability that still don't accept they can't do something.

To give you an example... acrobat Jennifer Bricker was born with some severe physical defects: her heart on the wrong side of her chest and she had no legs. But at an early age, she became fascinated with acrobatics and gymnastics. The idea of "Never say can't" was drummed into her by her parents, and when she was 11 she was so skilled that she competed in the Amateur Athletic Union Junior Olympics and came fourth in the Power Tumbling category. As an adult, she has performed all over the world as an acrobat and has been an inspiration to millions; all because she accepted her disability, refused to let it stop her and carried on regardless.

Like so many people competing in the Paralympics, it would be so easy not to bother trying to learn any sporting techniques. To just watch it on TV and dream about it. Yet even before the Paralympic Games was first held, in Rome in 1960, there were disabled athletes competing in the Olympic Games because they wouldn't take no for an answer if their disability was holding them back. One of my favourites is Károly Takács, a Hungarian army sergeant who was one of the world's top pistol shooters just before World War II. That is, until a faulty hand grenade exploded during a training exercise and destroyed his right hand. After that, he spent a year learning how to shoot with his left hand and turned up at the Hungarian National Pistol Shooting Championship in 1939. Everyone thought he'd just come to watch and support his old friends. Instead he competed, shooting with his left hand and he beat them all.

Although the next two Olympics were cancelled because

of World War II, he stuck with his shooting practice, and in the 1948 London Olympics he not only won a gold medal but set a world record in the rapid fire event. Four years later he got another gold. When his right hand was destroyed, he probably thought, "Oh well, that's that buggered then, no more shooting medals for me." But he shook off the thought and carried on.

Even nowadays, there are some athletes who could compete in the Paralympic Games but are also good enough at what they do to compete in the Olympics. The South African swimmer Natalie du Toit springs to mind. She started swimming at the age of 12 in South Africa and soon found out that she was pretty damn quick. At 17, she was good enough to only narrowly miss qualifying for the 2000 Sydney Olympics, so she relished the next four years of training so she'd be ready to compete in 2004 in Greece. That was until she was knocked off her motorbike and had to have her left leg amputated at the knee.

After a few months she was able to try swimming again but was unable to. She couldn't even swim 100 yards let alone a six-mile marathon swim. But she stuck at it. She practised anyway and ended up winning quite a few medals at the 2004 Paralympics. After four more years' practice, she qualified for the six-mile marathon swim at the 2008 Beijing Olympics with the able-bodied athletes and she even beat eight of them.

We can all learn from these people; we can all learn that we are going to suck at something for a while until we get good at it and that failure IS an option.

It's often said that accepting that you have a problem is the first step in overcoming it. Not all things can be overcome though; some things just need to be accepted and worked with. But no matter what you have to do, whether you need to learn to accept your imperfections and work with them or to recognise your flaws and learn to overcome them, we need some self-compassion.

Self-compassion is the foundation of self-esteem. Before thinking of ourselves favourably, as we would if we had high self-esteem, we need a solid acceptance of whom we are first. Without it, high self-esteem can cause more problems than it solves, such as narcissism and aggressive defensiveness.

Self-compassion doesn't even necessitate that we have to think of ourselves particularly favourably, and it certainly doesn't require us to see ourselves as better than someone else. Instead, the positive emotions of self-compassion will be there exactly when self-esteem is threatened; when we screw up or don't meet our own expectations.

If you think you don't like yourself enough to accept yourself, then ask yourself this question: "Do you really not like yourself or do you not like an ASPECT of yourself?" Because you don't have to like everything about yourself, and more importantly, you don't have to hate everything about yourself just because of one aspect. Is it actually just your fat bum that you don't like? Is it your selfishness that you don't like? That's fine. If there's something that you want to change, then maybe you can and maybe you can't. Maybe you don't even need to though.

ACCEPTING HOW YOU LOOK

A common thing that clients will often say to me is that they hate the way that they look and they hate looking in the mirror. Men will occasionally say this but it's more often a woman. In the absence of something more sinister, like body dysmorphic disorder, a great way to get used to the way that you look and to begin to accept yourself for who you are is to get in front of a mirror and look at yourself. If you fall into this category, then strip off the clothes, make-up and jewellery and stand in front of a mirror and get used to seeing what you look like.

EXERCISE

- Examine the nose that you keep telling yourself that you hate, look at your eyes and your hair (or lack of it).

- Use a full-length mirror if you can and embrace and accept what your body looks like.

- It's tempting to judge yourself when you're doing this at first but stop yourself if you do. You're not doing this to learn to judge yourself; you're doing this to learn to accept yourself.

- If you feel it's appropriate, talk to yourself. Say things like: "I accept myself the way that I am."

- Be compassionate rather than judgemental for a change and try saying things like: "I accept my body the way it is," or "I accept my tummy/nose/ receding hairline just the way it is."

- If you find that you don't believe yourself and you continue to be judgemental, you may need to insert the word "can" into the affirmation at first. "I CAN accept myself the way that I am," or "I CAN accept my body the way it is."

- You might find this can be quite uncomfortable as you begin to realise just how critical you may have been towards yourself in the past.

Journal Suggestions

1. What can you learn from your biggest mistakes?

2. What are the thoughts you'd most like to be rid of?

3. When do you feel the most alive?

4. What are the emotions you'd most like to be rid of?

5. When do you feel the most drained?

6. What are the memories you'd most like to be rid of?

7. What upsets you the most about life?

8. What are the behaviours you'd most like to be rid of?

Chapter Six:

Happy Body, Happy Mind

The Mind/Body Connection

In some languages, the word 'mind' is the same as it is for 'brain', but in English we've created this dualist attitude which infers that we have a lump of meat in our head called a brain, that does all this fancy signal-sending to help us navigate through life, and it is separate from our consciousness, which is widely referred to as the 'mind'.

It isn't.

Your brain IS your mind and therefore your mind is part of your body, so when people talk about the connection between mind and body, it shouldn't come as a surprise that thinking about the possibility of an itch on the tip of your nose right now will make the tip of your nose itch. So give it a little scratch and let's carry on, shall we?

Now that you know that your mind and body are one and the same, you might find that you can learn some of the tricks that we play on ourselves that can lead us to behaving in ways that can either help us or hinder us. Being aware of these things and having a good insight into how our psychology influences our behaviour, as well as how our behaviour influences our psychology, even at an unconscious level, can be very useful.

Just as your mood can influence your body language, reversely, the way that you use your body can influence your mood.

We all know that being happy makes you smile, and feeling depressed makes you slump your shoulders, but can we actually work it the other way around? Is there some sort of coded instinct inside all of us that creates a feeling based on something so simple as an expression? We do know that certain expressions are instinctive; toddlers that were blind from birth and have never seen someone pulling faces will still pull the same expressions as children that can see.

These expressions would have come about long before our prehistoric ancestors could even use language. Even all these years later, apes that haven't developed language will still bare their teeth when angry to let everyone know to keep out of their way. In the modern world, we can look at someone's body language and fairly accurately predict how they may be feeling. If they strut like John Travolta in the opening scene of *Saturday Night Fever*, we don't need Barry Gibb to tell us that "He's a woman's man with no time to talk". Similarly, if someone is standing in a corner at a party staring at the floor, protecting their vulnerable internal organs with their hands on their stomach and unable to make eye contact with anyone, then they're feeling a bit nervous.

As every method actor on stage and screen will tell you, if you act an emotion, you can feel an emotion, so by sitting up straight and smiling, can we really move from a miserable feeling into a happy one? Well, it certainly looks like it.

In one famous experiment conducted at the University of Mannheim in Germany,[46] volunteers were asked to underline vowels in sentences and draw some straight lines, before then rating the funniness of some Gary Larson's The Far Side cartoons. They were told that it was to investigate how someone who has recently lost the use of their hands might respond, so some participants were asked to hold a pencil in their mouths and some were asked to hold the pencil in their non-dominant hand. But in true scientific con-artistry, half of the pencil-in-mouth group were told that they had to hold the pencil in their teeth and that it mustn't touch their lips, and the other half were told to hold the pencil between their lips and that it mustn't touch their teeth.

This forced half of the pencil-in-mouth group to smile and the other half to frown. The results showed that by forcing your facial muscles to smile you can dramatically change the way that you feel. The participants were all shown the same cartoons, but across the board the volunteers whose faces had been forced into a smile found the cartoons funnier than those that had just used their other hand. And those who had been forced to frown found it less funny than the group holding the pencils in their non-dominant hands.

Further research shows that simply using your facial expressions to act 'as if' you are feeling particular emotions, like happiness, anger and sadness, influences you even after you've stopped acting.[47] So the positive influence of the smile doesn't immediately fade away; it sticks around for quite some considerable time.

It's been named the 'facial feedback hypothesis' and it has even been shown to have the same effect when the muscles for frowning are disabled with Botox injections.[48] That study, carried out at the University of Basel in Switzerland, included people who had quite major depression and had been unresponsive to anti-depressant medication. Half of them had injections of Botox and the other half received placebo injections of saline fluid. Six weeks after just a single dose, everyone came back and was assessed for their depressive symptoms using the infamous, but desperately gloomy, Hamilton Depression Rating Scale. Often abbreviated to HAM-D, this questionnaire is used to rate the severity of depression by assessing such things as a patient's mood, their feelings of guilt, suicide ideation, insomnia and anxiety. Popular since the early 1960s, it has had many different revisions over the years. Originally comprising only 17 questions, it now has 29 and takes around 20 minutes to answer, and it is used all over the world as a way of monitoring or diagnosing someone's depression. What the University of Basel researchers found was that the people who had received Botox injections to disable frowns experienced a 47% decrease in their depressive symptoms, compared to just 9% in the placebo group.

As for sitting up straight, it turns out that it's not just a way of making a good impression. Research findings[49] from dozens and dozens of studies back up what has been theorised for decades, showing that holding yourself in positive poses improves your confidence and mood. People who slouch feel powerless and people who stand tall feel powerful.[50] The research even showed that standing with your hands on your hips for a few minutes prior to a job interview means that you perform better and are more likely to be offered the job.

EXERCISE

BODY LANGUAGE TIP

Once per hour, take your thoughts to your body to see what sort of signals you're creating.

- Recognise that these signals aren't just being put out there to the world, they're also being fed back and acted upon by your own mind.

- Check if you're slouching.

- Check if you're frowning.

- Sit up straight.

- Smile.

- Smile with your eyes. A fake, forced smile (often amusingly referred to as a Pan Am smile after the now defunct airline and its superficially smiley flight attendants) just uses the cheek muscles, whereas a real smile (referred to as a Duchenne smile, after the French neurologist Guillaume Duchenne who first noticed this effect) also pulls on the muscles that close our eyes slightly, creating crow's feet. It's no coincidence that we often call these features 'laughter lines'.

It's useful not to wait until you're feeling low to do this. Do it anyway. Encourage a confident body posture to become a habit by deliberately taking your thoughts to your body once per hour to see how you're holding yourself, and if you need to act happier, then act happier.

With some issues that I treat, confidence for example, mentally pretending to be something that you're not can cause you to move further and further away from your goal. But when it comes to being happy, if you physically act as if you are, it can genuinely bring you closer to the real thing, but only if you do it properly.

Lying to yourself isn't likely to help. Saying to yourself, "I am so happy, my life is perfect," when you know full well it isn't, could make you feel worse rather than better, because it's usually followed up with, "Who am I kidding?" There are actions and behaviours that not only tell the external world how bad you're feeling, but also tell yourself. If you want to bring yourself down then speaking slowly, mumbling and wearing dull clothes will do just that as you emotionally respond to the way you treat yourself.

If you know that you look scruffy, but your self-esteem is too low to think that anyone cares what you look like, then going out will make you feel worse. But making some effort with your appearance, maybe also wearing brighter clothes and using your hands a little when speaking will help. Smiling when you meet someone and speaking in a jolly fashion are great ways of improving the way that you feel too. If you know that you've made an effort to show yourself and the world that you can be happier, then you will be able to put the ideas in this book into practice by finding a nice middle ground between being overly confident and under-confident, just by treating your body with respect because your brain is listening to how you treat it.

Which brings me on to the surprising benefits to improving mental health: physical health.

It's long been noted by doctors that there seems to be a correlation between poor mental health and poor physical health. Stress is known to have quite a negative effect on how quickly wounds heal, for example. And so a lot of studies have been undertaken over the years to look at it from the opposite way round. Can improving mental health have a positive effect on our body?

Recently Edward F. Diener, a professor of psychology at the University of Utah, oversaw a team who squinted at dozens of previous studies to confirm whether or not the previous experiments had been undertaken correctly. They concluded that yes, a happy mindset does have a positive effect upon our health.[51] This has been proven even in people recovering from surgery. Patients who are taught stress management techniques, guided imagery, or even those simple diaphragmatic breathing exercises from earlier on are known to heal faster. In one study from the University of Auckland,[52] 60 patients due to have their gall bladder removed at a local hospital were randomly split into two groups. Half of them received no extra support than is usual, but the other half also had a 45-minute session to learn de-stress techniques which included relaxation, guided imagery and also some relaxation CDs to take away and listen to for three days before the surgery and for seven days after their surgery. Both groups of patients had small plastic tubes inserted into their surgical wound during the operation which would then be removed seven days later. These tubes would collect deposits of hydroxyproline, a major component of the protein collagen and a perfect indication of how quickly a wound is being repaired. The experiment showed that patients who had been practising relaxation exercises had 95% more hydroxyproline in their wound, showing that learning to cope with stress can have a huge impact on how our bodies heal.

Dozens of previous studies have shown there to be a correlation between being happy and being healthy, but in a lot of cases we don't really know which direction the correlation flows in. Is it that being happy makes you more likely to be healthy or that being healthy makes you more likely to be happy? The consensus of opinion in the world of psychology seems to be that it's a bit of both. Yes, less anxiety and depression is going to have a positive effect upon your health. But feeling comfortable in your own skin is going to improve your wellbeing. And there are two ways to do that: you either accept the things you can't change or change the things you can't accept.

When people come to me as a hypnotherapist for help with weight loss, there are plenty of times that the client doesn't really need to lose much weight, if any. Often all they're looking for is how to be happy, and they think that by losing weight they would improve their confidence and be happier. So I teach them how to be more confident and happier, and any weight loss is a nice side effect. Us therapists find that to only teach clients about weight loss is not a very successful method. But, equally, to only teach about emotional wellbeing is not such a good idea either. You can teach an overweight person to love their body and embrace their shape but they might still get diabetes.

As with many things in life, you need to find a middle

ground between doing too little of something and doing too much. If you like pizza and eat it every day then it will have a negative effect on your happiness. If you like pizza and don't eat it at all, then it will also have a negative effect on your happiness. One of the first things I say to my weight loss clients is the good news that they'll never need to go on a diet ever again, because the changes they are going to make are not temporary. They're learning how to permanently think and behave differently, to create new habits and new behaviours that will stay with them for the rest of their lives.

The Best Medicine

Imagine that you could lose weight, have control over anxiety and depression, delay the onset of the ageing process and improve your brain power, all without taking any pills and without making any extra trips to the doctor. Wouldn't that be amazing?

Well, guess what? You can do those things. All the research conclusively proves it, and the secret is simple. It's just that people don't like to hear it, because the secret is nothing more than this: Exercise!

If a cheap pill came out on the market that could do all that, and with no negative side effects, we'd probably all be taking it. But the word 'exercise' tends to make us recoil in horror. After all, it takes effort! So what does it take for us to wake up and start doing it? Diabetes? Massive weight gain? A heart attack? At what point should we begin thinking about making exercise a part of our lives? It should be when we realise how good it can make us feel. But usually it's when we finally acknowledge how bad we're feeling and that we have no choice but to do something about it... when it's almost too late. It's very odd how us humans behave sometimes, how we so easily give in to the pull of instant gratification. Sitting down and watching brain-numbing TV shows just for the sake of it still feels better in the short term than going out for a brisk walk does, even though we know that in the long term the brisk walk will make us feel better than watching *Love Island* ever will.

In his book *Live Your Dreams*, Les Brown wrote a great little story that goes like this.

There was a young man walking down the street who happened to see an old man sitting on his porch. Next to the old man was his dog, who was whining and whimpering. The young man asked the old man, "What's wrong with your dog?" The old man said, "He's lying on a nail." The young man asked, "Lying on a nail? Well why doesn't he get up?" The old man then replied, "It's not hurting badly enough."

This attitude is one of the main reasons why people are resistant to making changes in their lives; they are not in enough pain to warrant all the effort it would take to get up off their nail and sit somewhere else. It's really not an exaggeration that exercise can do all the things I mentioned earlier, and hundreds and hundreds of research papers published within the last 15 years have shown it. If you don't believe me and you fancy some light reading, Julia Basso and Wendy Suzuki of New York University list 273 different studies in their review article 'The Effects of Acute Exercise on Mood, Cognition, Neurophysiology, and Neurochemical Pathways: A Review.' It was published in the journal *Brain Plasticity* in March 2017.[53] They concluded that the exciting potential for exercise is not only in addressing conditions where attention and mood may be compromised such as with ageing, ADHD and depression, but also its ability to enhance attention, mood and stress resistance in everyone else too. The footnotes at the very end of this book tell you where to find the studies and experiments that I talk about, so if you want to investigate anything further, you know where to look.

In some cases, exercise has been shown to cut the prevalence of the symptoms of anxiety in half! Don't get me wrong – there's nothing wrong with taking medication, but if you can achieve the same effects through exercise, you build confidence in your own ability to cope. And teaching the brain that we can survive is crucial to overcoming anxiety.

A landmark study into depression at Duke University even found that exercise worked better than medication can over the long term. Unlike anti-depressants, exercise doesn't selectively influence anything as medication would. Exercise simply adjusts the brain's chemistry so as to restore normality. It allows the brain to function with less effort so that we have greater resilience to put into place the ideas scattered throughout this book. It makes it easier for us to remember positive things and break out of the pessimistic patterns of depression. It also serves as proof that we can take the initiative to change something, which is great for our confidence.

As for ageing, getting old is unavoidable, but falling apart is not. Exercise is one of the few ways that we can counter the process of ageing. Exercise reverses cell deterioration, strengthens the cardiovascular system, boosts the immune system, fortifies bones and fosters neuroplasticity, which improves your brain's ability to learn, remember and execute higher thought processes.

Who would not want to do this? Only thing is, what if we lack the motivation? What if we find that there's always something else to do instead? Well, there always will be until you change your mindset, and that's why I talk about exercise so much in my consulting room, because it is no exaggeration that if you change your mindset then you can change your life, and it doesn't even need to be that difficult.

In one study conducted at the University of Virginia,[54] volunteers were asked to include some ten-minute exercise routines into their day. After three weeks of doing them three times per day, the participants' aerobic fitness was equal to that of people 10 to 15 years younger than them. And their strength, muscular endurance and flexibility were equal to those of people up to 20 years younger.

So in order to get fitter, you don't really have to join a gym – exercise isn't a commodity that you have to buy. You don't have to pay to take the stairs instead of an escalator at a shopping centre or walk to the shop for a pint of milk instead of driving. Any movement is going to be better than nothing at all, but we often have this mindset that exercise is an all-or-nothing process. As if we must be sweating for half an hour for it to be classed as exercise, but it's not true.

One twin can even be healthier than the other just because they fidget a bit,[55] as was shown by Claude Bouchard, Professor and Director of the Human Genomics Laboratory at Pennington Biomedical Research Center, Louisiana. Bouchard is a scientist who studies the genetics of fitness and obesity, and back in 1997 he studied twins as a way to try and isolate a genetic marker for obesity. What he found was a genetic component to how much someone may undertake spontaneous physical activities, including fidgeting. Identical twins were likely to be as fidgety as each other whereas fraternal (non-identical twins) were just as likely to be different from each other in the fidgeting department. It confirmed something that had been first spotted back in 1986 by Dr. Eric Ravussin, who helped to build the first human respiratory chamber in Lausanne, Switzerland before later building his own at The National Institute of Diabetes and Digestive and Kidney Diseases in Phoenix, Arizona. This chamber was a room that could accurately measure the energy output of everything from using an exercise bike to lying on a bed.[56] the results showed a huge difference in the amount of calories that people can burn off. Some subjects burned as few as 1,300 calories in one 24-hour period, while others burned as much as 3,600 calories over 24 hours. Ravussin and his team have shown us that if someone can burn more calories just because when they're bored they play cards rather than watch TV, then doing a few squats while waiting for the kettle to boil is actually quite a lot better than doing nothing.

Problems tend to occur when people try too hard to keep fit. If what you plan to do seems unrealistic, then you won't stick at it. Simply including more movement into your day is going to teach your body that everything is great and will have a positive effect on your mood.

QUICK EXERCISES FOR BEGINNERS

Exercising doesn't have to take up too much of your life – doing something for just ten minutes every other day is absolutely fine. What's important is finding out what works for you. One size does not fit all, and if that means that in those ten minutes you exercise for 30 seconds and then rest for 30 seconds that's fine. Eventually you'll be able to do something for a full minute and only need 15 seconds to recover. In doing so, you might find that the work you do in that full minute gets more intense with every week that goes by.

Whichever exercises you end up doing, start by warming up for two minutes in whichever way you prefer. You might want to try one of the three ideas below:

EXERCISE

- Stand up straight and swing each arm backwards, one after another, as though you were swimming backstroke.

- Jog or simply march on the spot for 30 seconds.

- Stand up straight and bring each knee up as high as you need to so as to touch it with your opposite hand.

- Once your muscles have warmed up a bit, you can push yourself a little further, and in less time than it would probably take you to drive to your gym, you can have a workout that will not only boost your physical state, but also your mental state too. So, get your heart pumping for a short period, no longer than 60 seconds and then rest for a while – between ten seconds and 30 seconds is fine depending on how long you'd sustained the exercise but there are no rules to this – just do what you feel comfortable with. Here are some suggestions:

- Jumping Jacks. Stand with your feet hip-width apart and your arms at your sides. Raise your

EXERCISE

arms above your head and at the same time jump your feet apart. Repeat as fast as you can.

- Side Step Jacks. If a normal Jumping Jack is a bit hard for you, try stepping side to side while raising your arms instead.

- Star Jumps. Stand with your feet shoulder-width apart and your arms at your sides. Bend your knees and begin to squat down before jumping up as quickly as you can, making a star shape with your arms and legs.

- Use the stairs. It might sound simple but running up and down the stairs as quickly as you can for 60 seconds is going to get your heart pounding a lot more than you might have expected.

- On the spot jogging. Jog on the spot as fast as possible by bringing your knees up as high as you can.

I know it might not sound much, but between ten and 15 minutes of exercise every other day is all you need to do to have quite a serious impact.

Instinctive Eating

Ask yourself: "Why do I eat?" The sensible answer is that you eat because you get hungry, but I'm willing to bet that you eat something on plenty of occasions whether you're hungry or not. I'm willing to bet that you regularly eat something simply because it's right there in front of you. I'm also willing to bet that with most of your meals you could get halfway through, find that you're no longer hungry and could stop and come back to the rest of it later on if you get hungry again.

But we have habits and routines that our brain expects us to perform, and it makes us feel slightly anxious when we don't perform them. I have lots of clients who tell me that they NEVER leave food on their plate when they've finished a meal, as if the exact amount of food they needed in that moment was the exact amount that was served up. That's too much of a coincidence, isn't it? What, the exact amount? Not a single forkful too much? There are plenty of times that we eat when we don't need to, often down to the automatic and unconscious signals that our brain is sending that lead to us going back to a buffet for another sausage roll or mindlessly dig into the bag of Maltesers while watching a film.

In April 2015 in the UK, a law became fully implemented to protect the public from cigarette promotion by forcing all retailers to hide their tobacco products from public view. Shop owners can show you a paper list of what they sell but they can't legally show the display to you. The Government did this because research has consistently shown that if something's out of sight it's also out of mind. It's the same psychological process that is in place when you see a dessert menu in a restaurant. Often you're just too full to even think about a dessert, but if the restaurant actually brings a trolley round and shows you the desserts available, not only are you more likely to choose one but also you're happy to pay more for it according to research at the California Institute of Technology.[57] In a series of experiments in 2010, they showed that seeing the actual item, rather than just an item on a menu, increased how much someone would be willing to pay for it by as much as 61%. If we can see it, then we want it all the more. The same applies at home. If you've got snacks on display in your kitchen, don't be surprised if you eat them whether you're hungry or not. After all, the first bite is with the eye. But it turns out it's not just the first bite; it's often every bite.

Results of many experiments show that our level of satisfaction is not linked to how much we ate, but rather that we finished what was put in front of us. Researchers at Cornell University[58] offered a group of students a free lunch for several weeks. Unbeknown to the students, everything they ate was measured and weighed. Each week the amount was increased yet the students continued to eat whether they were satisfied or not.

Similarly, in 2005 Brian Wansink from Cornell University published findings from an amusing experiment[59] in which groups of people were seated at a table with bowls of soup. Everyone was told that they could eat as much as they wanted for 20 minutes, and if a bowl of soup was reduced to just a quarter left then another serving of creamy tomato soup would be ladled in for them. Half of the group had normal bowls, but the other half had bowls that were self-refilling (they were connected through a 2cm hole in the bottom of the bowl with food-grade tubing to a cauldron at the other end of the table). Through a gravity-feed mechanism they would slowly and unnoticeably receive extra soup. Those with the self-refilling bowls ate an average of 73% more soup, but interestingly, they didn't realise. They didn't believe that they had eaten more and nor did they rate themselves as any more satisfied than the other group did. They even estimated that they had eaten 140 fewer calories than they actually did, showing that we use our eyes not our stomachs as a reference to how satisfied we are.

So if you're part of the 'clean plate brigade', bear this experiment in mind and you may well discover that you can be equally satisfied with your meals if you just use slightly smaller plates.

Another popular answer to the question: "Why do I eat?" is because of emotions. We eat because we're bored; we eat because we're stressed; we eat because we're depressed. This is no secret, but the extent to which our eating habits are influenced by even slight emotional shifts is quite surprising. In a 2013 experiment,[60] at the University of Miami, researchers asked people to take part in a taste test for a new kind of M&M sweet. Half of them were given a cupful of the supposed new version and were told that the secret ingredient was a luxury, high-calorie chocolate.

The other half also received a cup of M&M's, but they were told that their new chocolate was low-calorie. All of the participants were told that they could eat as many as they wanted so as to fill in a taste test evaluation form.

The truth of the matter was that there were no differences at all in the M&M's; the researchers were actually measuring how many sweets they consumed after they had been exposed to posters that displayed either neutral sentences or sentences related to struggle and adversity. I chatted with Dr. Anthony Salerno, who designed the study, and he explained to me how the experiment was undertaken. He created two large posters – nothing fancy just a large white piece of paper with black writing on it. One poster had these six sentences written on it:

Life is a Game of Survival
Withstand Whatever You Can
The Hunter Showed Great Persistence
A Shortfall Signals the End
The Long Period of Struggle Awaits Us
She Could Deal With Adversity

The other poster had the same sentence structure, but with one key word changed. This time it said:

Life is a Game of Chess
Consider Whatever You Can
The Hunter Showed Great Patience
A Conclusion Signals the End
The Long Period of Pause Awaits Us
She Could Deal With Anonymity

The six key words from each sentence were in a slightly larger font size and the posters were positioned against a wall six feet away from the tasting table, directly across from participants.

The people who were primed to think about the first set of

sentences, about environmental harshness, ate 70% more of the 'luxury' M&M's than the people eating the "low-calorie' M&M's. In the control group, which had posters with neutral words on display, they both ate the same amount whether they thought they were high-calorie or not and still scoffed far less than their unconsciously anxious counterparts.

Many people will talk about how they find that they desire unhealthier food when they're stressed, but this experiment shows us that we don't need much extra stress at all for us to be influenced into making unhealthier choices. We might need to pay more attention to why we make the choices we do sometimes, just in case it's not really hunger we're experiencing. Our instincts to desire high-calorie food during harsh times goes back thousands of years, but it's still the blink of an eye really when compared to the evolution and migration of the human race, so it's no surprise that thinking about tough times, even for just a fraction of a second, influences us.

Because everyone was actually eating the same M&M's and because the neutral groups both ate the same quantity, you can see that it wasn't how the sweets actually tasted that caused them to eat more, but rather it was the instinctive desire for greater calories. And all it took was a poster to be placed six feet away from them, with a few negative sentences on, to encourage them to consume more. Next time you put the news on the TV, see how many negative sentences you're being exposed to and don't be surprised if you end up fancying chocolate rather than a glass of water.

Weight Loss Tips

Weight gain is, without question, a big problem. In the UK, 15 million people are classed as overweight, and a huge percentage of those people will have dieted, failed, dieted again and failed again.

Adding some new habits to your daily routine can facilitate weight loss, and help you to reach your goal easily and permanently. Achieving a healthy weight is easier to accomplish when you simply follow a series of small steps and don't think about the big picture.

A great start will be to use some of the weight loss ideas identified in this chapter. Now, there's nothing new under the sun and you may well already know that these ideas would be useful, but I think that having a better understanding of the research that proves these ideas work should give you the extra optimism to stick at it.

The issue is that in the modern age we have got used to pressing a button to make something work, taking a pill to have an almost immediate effect on our physical problems and wanting everything NOW! This is why the Atkins diet, the cabbage soup diet and most other fad diets become popular, because they promise to help people to lose weight fast.

But do they work permanently? No. We just end up going straight back to our 'before we dieted' diet and put it all back on… and more! Our bodies aren't built for just cabbage soup and neither are our minds. As anyone who has ever decided to cut something out of their life will tell you, you will want whatever you gave up originally all the more!

There is no magic pill that can make you lose weight in

an instant. There is a lot going on in your mind and body and it ALL needs tackling before you can keep the weight off forever.

So how do we do it?

The best way for most people to lose weight is to eat a little less and move about a little bit more. Problems occur when the diet that people choose is unrealistic, whether that's because it doesn't suit them or they don't suit it. Either way, something needs to change, otherwise the diet makes them feel as if they're denying themselves of too much.

When clients come to me for weight loss help, the amount they say they want to lose varies from person to person. Some say one stone, some say ten stone. They might all have a different goal in mind but they all have one thing in common. They don't feel confident that they can achieve it without help, hence why they've come to see me. Not feeling that their goal is realistic is one of the biggest issues that we need to tackle first, and we do that by breaking their goal down into smaller goals.

The truth is that no matter how much weight they ultimately want to lose, it always starts with a small amount. With most people it can be as little as two pounds. They might need to lose those two pounds more than once, but with their goal always being just two pounds, then it feels more realistic, because they feel confident that they can do that.

If you're in a similar position, then please recognise that big goals such as five stone are OK to imagine when looking for motivation, but you need to bear in mind that there are increments in between first.

If you want to lose five stone, it will seem a long way off when you weigh yourself and see very little change, and this is likely to undo all the motivation you might have. The important thing for permanent weight loss is that it needs to be done slowly. Because of this, one of the first things you might need to learn is patience.

Our generation is so used to paying for things on credit cards rather than saving up that we are losing touch with the truth that there are some things that we need to wait for.

Weight loss is most definitely one of them. You're not looking for the quickest way; you're looking for the most effective.

Clients often tell me that they've been on a diet for as much as 20 years and yet every time they lose weight it just sucks itself back on again, and the circle of life continues.

It was Albert Einstein who is so often quoted as saying, "The definition of insanity is doing the same thing over and over again and expecting different results." We don't need to be a Nobel Prize-winning physicist to know this, though.

We can clearly see from the experiments I mentioned earlier that we don't feel any difference in satisfaction when we give ourselves healthy-size portions or unhealthy portions. So start by giving yourself a smaller portion of food rather than dramatically changing what you eat, and you will enjoy your food just as much yet consume fewer calories. The only reason that this might be difficult is simply down to bad habits. So learn a new habit like eating a smaller portion or leaving food on your plate every time and all will be well. Research has shown time and again that smaller plates look as if they contain more food than larger plates do, even when the amount of food is exactly the same. Similarly, experiments have shown that eating with smaller cutlery encourages you to take smaller mouthfuls of food.[61]

Psychology professor Dr. Paul Rozin set out two bowls of sweets in an apartment building's lobby. He hung a sign that said: "Help yourself – take as much as you want." And everyone did, on their way in and out of the building. But they did not take an amount based on how hungry they were or how much they wanted a snack. Instead, each person took what they thought was one serving. If they came upon a bowl with a large serving spoon, they would take that amount, and eat all the sweets in that large serving. If they happened upon the other bowl with a much smaller spoon, they would use that spoon and eat the amount it contained. Hunger seemed to be irrelevant.

Another important factor in how much you enjoy your food is how quickly you eat it. Dr. Kathleen Melanson, Director of the Energy Metabolism Lab at the University of Rhode Island, USA, undertook an experiment into the correlation between satisfaction and the speed in which we eat.[62] Researchers gave a group of women a pasta meal; half of the women were given small cutlery and also were instructed to eat slowly by putting down the cutlery while they chewed, while the other half of the group were given larger cutlery and were told to eat quickly. When the women were interviewed after the meal, the fast eaters had eaten more calories and did not feel particularly satisfied, but the slow eaters had eaten less and felt fuller.

This is because it takes time for the stomach to send signals to the brain to tell it to feel satisfied, and because eating produces chemicals in the brain associated with pleasure. The signals, even when they do reach the brain, are often ignored because the brain is too busy producing the pleasure chemicals.

Eating slowly, chewing your food more and putting down your cutlery during mouthfuls do not prevent the pleasure chemicals being produced, yet these actions give the brain a chance to pick up on what the stomach is doing and allow feelings of satisfaction to occur.

However, issues with diet can tend to lie outside of how and what you're eating. One often overlooked reason for overeating can be a lack of adequate sleep. During the nights where we've had the correct amount needed, our bodies release a chemical called leptin, which is produced by fat cells and passes through the circulatory system to the brain. leptin signals the brain and lets it know when food has filled the body. But, as well as being an appetite suppressant, leptin also has some effect on body temperature, so it actually increases the amount of calories burned.

As was shown in studies at the University of Chicago in 2004,[63] by not sleeping enough we don't produce enough leptin. Mice that were bred not to produce leptin continually overate nonstop and soon became obese. When testing with humans, the researchers found that restricting the amount that volunteers slept led to an almost 20% drop in leptin levels in their blood.

Similarly, when we do not sleep properly, we overproduce a chemical called ghrelin, which not only increases feelings of hunger but also suppresses the amount of fat used by the adipose tissue and prevents the production of leptin. This implies that those with high levels of ghrelin in their bodies will not only feel hungrier than those with low levels, but may burn fat more slowly as well. So in short: ensure that you get enough sleep. I talk about sleep earlier in the book, but you will know if you are getting enough sleep if you are already awake when your alarm clock goes off. If your alarm clock is constantly waking you up, then you either need to go to bed earlier or learn how to fall asleep quicker.

QUICK HEALTH TIP

Is there a particular food that you just don't like?

Something that would make it easier for you to make healthier choices if you were to like it?

For me it was bananas. At one time I would take quite a few unhealthy snacks into work to scoff between clients, using the excuse that I needed something quick and easy to give me energy so that I didn't keep my clients waiting. It was a lie; I was just being greedy. So I decided to learn to like bananas. This is something that I probably never would have done had I not been a therapist who understood how behaviourism works. I knew that if you repeat something enough times you soon get used to it. But would that work with food? Yes, it turns out that it does. But it took a month of eating a banana every single day, whether I wanted it or not. Each week that went by I noticed that it was becoming easier to stomach, and around five weeks in, there was one particular day where we'd run out of bananas and I felt disappointed – I hadn't realised that I had been looking forward to eating it.

EXERCISE

Is there something that you could introduce?

- Pick a fruit or a vegetable that you don't like, and make the effort to eat some of it every single day.

- If you are really averse to the idea, or even phobic of new foods, then don't worry if you need to spit it out for the first couple of days, or even weeks if needs be. Tread gently with yourself and work your way up by taking it a step at a time. Start by only holding it in your mouth and then spitting it out. After a week of that, take the next step of chewing it a little before spitting it out. Eventually you'll be able to swallow some and eventually even learn to enjoy it.

- Have a read of some healthy recipes but instead of discounting the ones that sound awful to you, have a think about what specific ingredient you don't like about it.

- Be patient. Trust in the process that runs through the whole of this book that if you do something enough times it will become second nature.

If you want to lose weight, one of the first things I suggest to people is to throw away the scales. Your actual weight is very subjective and is not really much of an indicator of how healthy you are anyway. The scales don't differentiate between muscle and fat and it's possible that as a person gets healthier with more muscular definition, their BMI score increases. This is simply because muscle weighs more than fat. Remember that Tom Cruise would have been classed as obese during the filming of the *Mission Impossible* films, because he was so fit and bulked up with muscle for the role. However, despite the fact that people know that muscle weighs more than fat, they continue to weigh themselves as a measurement of success.

If you're going to weigh yourself then at least do it very infrequently – monthly is probably a good idea. If you weigh yourself once per month you will be able to see the differences easier, and for those of you who weigh yourself multiple times per day (yes, these people do exist), it's going to come as a bit of a shock to you, but stick with it and you'll be fine.

Obsessing over the numbers on the scale will make the weight loss process feel like harder work than it should be. Bear in mind that our weight fluctuates for many different reasons, such as salt and carbohydrate intake, hormone levels and constipation. There are lots of reasons why you may actually be doing a lot of the right things, but are not necessarily seeing it on the scales. Judging yourself because you thought you'd done well but the scales seem to tell you that you didn't, often causes people to give up, so throw them away if you like.

If you want to measure something, I suggest using a flimsy tailor's tape measure and measuring the bits of you that you'd like to be slimmer, because that's what people tend to mean when they say they want to lose weight. They want to be slimmer, not lighter. They want their clothes to fit them better and the numbers on a scale won't show that. So measure your arms, your waist your thighs, whatever. Make a note of them and come back to it in one month's time after implementing the ideas in this chapter. Even if it's only a few centimetres here or half an inch there it doesn't matter, you're moving in the right direction and can be optimistic that you're doing the right thing.

WEIGHT LOSS QUESTIONS

Answering these questions can give you some clarity into the deeper reasons as to why you want to lose weight. They can help you to identify what your stumbling blocks might be so that you can find solutions for them. You need to be truly honest with yourself, though; in doing so, you prove to yourself that you are both ready for change and committed to it.

So, grab a pen and paper and go into as much detail as you feel you need to.

1. Why do you want to lose weight? What sort of feelings would being slimmer give you? How would your life be different?
2. Why have you been unable to lose weight or maintain your weight loss in the past? Why have you failed? Think back and replay what went wrong. What were the triggers, the stumbling blocks, the people, places and attitudes that took you off course?

3. What are the main things causing you stress in your life right now? Are there any emotional reasons that contribute to overeating? List feelings and emotional reactions that lead you to make bad choices. Does feeling underappreciated at work drive you to eat chocolate as a way of trying to make you feel better? Does having an argument with a friend encourage you to try and calm down with a tub of ice cream? Are you unhappy with some aspect of your career, relationship or friends?

4. What are you really hungry for? What's the one thing in your life that hasn't come your way?

5. Do you have negative beliefs about trying to lose weight? Finish these sentences: "I would exercise more, but…" "I would eat healthier, but…" Find out what it is that's been holding you back.

6. Do you have any fears about losing weight? Such as being afraid of getting more attention; after all, it's not for everyone. Or do you have a fear of failure?

7. What are some more appropriate things you can do instead of turning to food when bored, stressed or feeling emotional?

There's a lot that can be done in 15 minutes that will improve your physical health, whether that's playing Swingball, pushing a lawnmower or swinging some kettlebells around the front room – it's all good for you. But if you want some specific exercises to do before jumping in the shower every morning, it's a good idea to try some varied ones. Rather than 15 minutes of press-ups, it would be more engaging to do just 30 seconds of press-ups, even if you have to do them on your knees at first. Have a rest for 30 seconds and then do some sit-ups for 30 seconds. Find things that work for you; you can do anything (within reason) as long as it gets your heart pumping, and it's absolutely fine to rest for half a minute (or longer if you need to) between short bursts of exercise.

The only thing to bear in mind is that we have a bit of a quirk to our psychology that means we usually overestimate the amount of calories burned when exercising and underestimate the calories consumed in a snack or a meal, so don't think that 15 minutes of exercise means you can eat a Mars bar as a treat – that's not really how it works!

Journal Suggestions

1. If your body could talk, what would it say?

2. When do you remember feeling at your healthiest?

3. What would be your stumbling blocks to getting fitter?

Chapter Seven

Get Yourself Connected

Social Connections

Relative to our body size, humans have the largest brain in the animal kingdom. The usual effects of evolution show brain size only increases if the rest of the body is increasing too, yet this rule goes right out of the window for us. We are a bit of an anomaly in that our brains are way bigger than they should be. Around seven million years ago, one set of our ancestors thought that the trees were the best place to hang out and another set fancied the idea of being down on the ground, and so we went our separate ways. The tree dwellers' brains didn't change, but ours tripled in size. Scientists have long pondered why we have this larger, hungrier brain. It only makes up around 2% of our body mass, yet it uses up more than 20% of our blood flow and oxygen supply. In comparison, the brains of other primates consume only 7%, so that more energy can be directed to their muscles. This is why you should never underestimate the strength of a chimp. You might well win if you play it at chess, but it will almost certainly beat you in an arm wrestle.

One very popular theory as to why our brains have become bigger than expected is down to developing social skills. Anthropologists think that the first hominids with brains as big as ours, Homo heidelbergensis, showed up in Africa around 700,000 years ago. They appear to be the common ancestor of both modern humans and Neanderthals. They also seem to be the first hominids to have worked together to hunt, had central campsites, and they may even have been the first of our kind to bury their dead.

In order to function as a society, we began to get quite good at empathising, seeing things from someone else's perspective and generally taking other people into consideration when making decisions. Natural selection favoured it, so it became a dominant factor in our evolution, and here we are all these years later still possessing these instincts to work together. But they are instincts that we can ignore if we choose to. If we like, we can sit at home on our own, not see anyone and still be happy people.

But, according to research by Matthew Lieberman, a professor of biobehavioral sciences at the University of California,[64] the default mode our brain goes into, when not distracted by anything else, is one that is also used for social thinking or making sense of other people and ourselves. We know this from analysing brain activity in various situations and then comparing them. The conclusion was that being part of society makes a happy brain.

Other studies have also found many correlations

between social functioning and happiness, with one study undertaken at the University of Michigan[65] showing that a lack of social connections has an even greater negative effect upon our health than obesity, smoking and high blood pressure do.

Despite social connectedness apparently being just as important to our success in life as our need for food and shelter is, sociological research[66] shows that the former is declining at quite a disturbing pace. In modern society, we are less likely to volunteer, less likely to have dinner parties and more likely to have fewer and fewer close friends with each year that goes by. In 1985, when people were asked how many friends they have that they would share a personal problem with, the most common number to come up with was three. By 2004, it had dropped to just one, with 25% of the people surveyed saying that they literally had nobody at all that they classed as a close friend.

QUICK TIP

Look for a local organisation to join, find your local Men In Sheds Club or Ladies Club if you want to stick with your own gender in a group. A quick search on your local council website for the community activities directory will give you a lot of local clubs and social groups to consider joining. You'll be surprised what goes on in your local area and they're always looking for new members.

Humans are increasingly denying ourselves something that is a fundamental reason for having not gone extinct – our social nature, and we are paying a price for it. Throughout the same time frame that social isolation has been increasing, our levels of happiness have been decreasing and the rates of depression and suicide have multiplied.

It's very odd that the more technology we have that allows us to connect to people, the less connected we actually become. Maybe virtual connections are just not quite good enough. On the surface, Facebook looks as if it would be a great idea. It provides a great resource for fulfilling our need for social connection. But, rather than enhancing our wellbeing, research findings suggest that Facebook may actually make us feel worse.[67]

A 2013 study from the University of Michigan Institute for Social Research[68] had researchers texting a quick survey five times per day to volunteers. In it, they asked a few questions including asking them to rate how they were feeling, how many times they'd used Facebook since the last text and how many times they'd had direct social interaction with people.

They also filled in a questionnaire before and after the two weeks over which the experiment took place so that they could get a baseline of their satisfaction in life. The researchers were easily able to predict the life satisfaction levels at the end of the study by analysing how frequently they'd used Facebook. The more people used it, the worse they felt the next time they text-messaged them and the more they used Facebook over two weeks, the more their life satisfaction levels declined.

But why does online social networking not make us happier when face-to-face networking does? Facebook only gives us glimpses into someone's world; glimpses that are at best filtered and at worst fabricated, to such an extent that it's become outside of the norm for someone to post something genuinely personal. For someone to write on Facebook how depressed they are, how they feel that their relationship is holding them back or that they feel unfulfilled with life is almost unheard of. Instead, people lie and say, "Couldn't be happier, chilling with my perfect man tonight after a great day at the office."

Really? I don't think so. If someone genuinely feels that good, they wouldn't be wasting their 'perfect chill time' with their partner by posting things on Facebook. No one's holiday pictures include the sickness and diarrhoea, the cockroaches or the drunken fight with the bus driver. Instead, they'll lie on their back and post a photo of their feet with the sea in the background instead, because that's what they want you to see.

If someone wants you to know something, question why. Is it to make them feel good? Is it to try and make you feel bad? Now, I'm not saying NEVER use it, but I am saying don't swap genuine interaction with a real human being for a like on a Facebook comment.

There's a time and a place for it. If you're bored, sitting around, waiting for your wife to come out of the changing rooms at Selfridges AGAIN, then that's not so bad, but don't let it replace something more useful. After all, your mobile phone has already replaced your camera, your CD player, even your bookshelf. It shouldn't also replace your connection with friends and family.

SOCIAL MEDIA DETOX

If you're feeling a little too dependent on social media to feel connected with the world, then you might consider taking a break from it. Think about implementing one of the following 'levels':

LEVEL ONE: Only use social media outside of working hours. If your work is a bit stressful or you need a distraction, you may need a better coping strategy than social media. Practise those diaphragmatic breathing exercises (see page 24) and take a quick walk. Go and get a drink of water and see how many people you can smile at or say hello to on your way to and from your desk.

LEVEL TWO: The same as level one, but also make a conscious effort to restrict how often you use social media outside of working hours too. Many people who use their phone for their social media updates say they find it hard to keep away from it in the evenings when they're at home. If this sounds like you, and you're in the habit of relaxing on the sofa watching TV at the same time as scrolling through Facebook, try keeping your phone in a different room. Or at least a good distance away from you, and make sure that it's out of sight. Only check it once per hour, and restrict yourself to just a few minutes before putting it out of sight.

LEVEL THREE: This time, add in the restriction that three nights per week you won't use social media at all. Turn off notifications, the banners on your phone's lock screen and audio alerts so you won't be reminded about it. Just watch what happens next, because I can pretty much guarantee that it will be nothing. Nothing will happen next. Nobody will be angry with you for not liking their posts and you won't miss out on anything.

LEVEL FOUR: Ignorance is bliss. Delete the app and maybe even consider deactivating your account. You can always go back to it if you need to in the future. There are occasions when it's a necessary evil, such as projects you work on that involve using Facebook Groups as a way of sharing information. If so, see which of the levels you feel you need and stick to it. In the meantime, get into the habit of keeping in touch with people you like and care about in a more genuine fashion. Call them, leave a voicemail message if they're busy so that they can hear your voice. You might find that they miss hearing from you as much as you miss them, and hearing your voice, even on voicemail, will help you both to feel connected.

Comfort Zones

A little bit of social anxiety can lead to a huge amount of loneliness if you're not careful, yet a cure for loneliness is obviously to get out there and meet people. So there's a cruel irony here that the side effects of the medicine can feel more painful than the problem. But it's not painful forever. By slowly and steadily stretching your comfort zone, you will learn the skills that give you confidence in social situations. But, interestingly, there is a big difference between being alone and being lonely, and plenty of people still feel connected with society even when they're not actually 'out there' connecting.

In the same way that it's possible to feel lonely in a crowd of people, it's also possible to feel connected when you're actually all alone. Social connection doesn't come from how many friends we have, but rather it comes from how we feel about the friends that we do have. It's our internal sense of connection towards them, whether they are actually with us or not. Just because they're not with you doesn't mean missing them has to be a bad thing. What is it about them that makes you miss them? Is it how much you enjoyed their company last time you were together? If so, remember that experience, and think about how you felt that day. Remember that how you think will influence how you feel, which influences how you behave, which then influences how you think, and round and round it goes. If you think about being alone, it can create the emotion of loneliness. The isolated feelings loneliness gives us means we can often feel disconnected from our friends, and then we are less likely to contact them, which gives us evidence that we're alone and round and round it goes.

I have many clients who hide away from the real world due to social anxiety and only chat online through video games or social media messaging. Some are OK with it and still feel happy and connected, but just as many do not. The difference between these two types of people who are seemingly doing the same thing but feeling opposite emotions interested me, so I dug deeper into their habits. When they described how they use social media there were big differences. The lonely people would just scroll through looking at other people's lives, sometimes with a sense of envy that made them feel isolated all the more. The not so lonely people were engaging more with their contacts in a variety of ways. Rather than just pushing the 'Like' button, they were commenting on posts and contributing to a connection that went multiple ways, and they used the website Nextdoor to chat about what was happening locally. They might not have had the confidence to make new face-to-face friends but they were more connected and happier than those who were just lurking on Facebook, watching everyone else making connections without them.

An online connection may well be better than nothing, though it's not better than the real thing. But to start talking with complete strangers in a pub takes either confidence or at least an ability to be able to handle anxiety. We need a strength of mind to prevent negative thinking that can come from worrying about what someone might think of us, and overcome any fear of silence that seems to come from not knowing how to start a conversation.

I remember reading some research showing that four seconds of silence in a conversation between strangers was enough to make someone say something just to fill the gap. On the fifth second, someone in the group would just blurt something banal out such as "Crikey – is that the time already!" or "I wonder what the weather's doing!"

More and more research backs up this assertion that feeling included in society wakes up the happy part of the brain.

Yet if you were to ask someone who is about to board a train whether they'd be happier to sit in silence and relax in their own thoughts or to chat with a stranger, they almost always say, "Sitting in silence, that would make me happier."

But would it? Well, no, it turns out that it wouldn't. In a series of experiments, put together by Nicholas Epley and Juliana Schroeder of the University of Chicago,[69] commuters at a train station were asked to do one of two things. In exchange for a Starbucks gift card they were asked to either talk to whomever was sitting next to them on their train journey or keep themselves to themselves and say nothing.

By the end of their journey, the commuters who had talked to a stranger reported having a more positive experience than those who had sat in silence. Repeating the experiment with buses and taxi journeys, and offering the commuters bananas and lottery tickets as a thank you for taking part, all yielded the same results. Most of the commuters predicted that they would be unhappy with chatting, yet their mood at the end of their journey was significantly greater than those that had sat in solitude. Interestingly, this happiness boost was the same for people who thought of themselves as introverts as it was for the extraverts, so it had nothing to do with any natural social skills they might have had.

But why were the commuters' predictions and their experiences so different? The researchers reported that commuters felt that they would have nothing in common with anyone and imagined that it would be difficult to start a conversation. They estimated that fewer than half of their fellow commuters would want to talk to them, whereas not a single person reported having been ignored, and the conversations were apparently consistently enjoyable. So the results went against everyone's expectations.

Because of 21st-century anxieties surrounding what people think of us, we avoid contact with other people and that may well make us feel worse. This fear is exacerbated if you already have a habit of feeling judged by everyone.

Fear of rejection is a big issue for many people, and an understandable one as, historically, to be banished from your village, tribe, herd or flock meant you were going to starve or be eaten. So, it's no surprise that the biggest fears that people seem to have are about making sure that they aren't rejected.

Just because there's an evolutionary benefit to fearing rejection or being judged, it doesn't mean we have to hold on to it. There's an evolutionary benefit to eating fat and sugar, but that doesn't mean we all do; it just means that we have to work a little harder to make the opposing behaviour second nature, but it can be done. So next time you take public transport, start a conversation with the person sitting next to you. Maybe ask them what they are up to that day or whether they had a busy weekend. Talk about the weather if you have to and let it lead into their opinion on the pedestrianisation of Norwich city centre. Small talk is OK, and while it may not be scintillating, it's still a great way to connect.

GET CHATTING

Chit chat, small talk or whatever else you want to call it might seem like a waste of time on the face of it. You're unlikely to make a good friendship with a total stranger on a bus so you might think, "What's the point?" But not only does it push the happy buttons in the brain, it also gives you some extra confidence that makes it easier to handle those sorts of situations again.

Ironically, modern technology seems to have created a world in which we increasingly crave genuine face-to-face connections, while at the same time stripping us of the skills we need to actually make it happen. If you fall into this category, getting better connected with society might mean you need to stretch your comfort zone a little.

Under-confident or shy characters will often take on a very backseat role when it comes to conversations, not just with strangers but even with people they already know. They simply wait for someone else to start a conversation, and so two shy people standing next to each other at a mutual friend's house party won't say a word to each other.

Someone needs to take the active role if you are to get some benefit from connecting with people. That person will probably have to be you, as 21st-century expectations are that everyone ignores each other. If someone starts a friendly conversation with you on the bus, then that's great – take the opportunity to engage and breathe a sigh of relief that it wasn't you that had to get the ball rolling. But unless they've got a copy of this book sticking out of their bag, there's a fair chance it will be you that starts the conversation.

Now, when we were at school and learning about these social conventions, things were different for us. It's quite normal for a ten-year-old to stand next to a complete stranger and say, "Do you like Spider-Man?" but for an adult? That's perhaps not a good idea. If the random stranger on the bus is wearing a T-shirt with "I Love DC Comics" on it, then maybe starting a conversation about which Marvel characters they might like too is probably OK. But in most situations, outside of a playground, it means having to think about it first. So here are my tips for starting conversations:

EXERCISE

- Don't try too hard. Be relaxed about it and spend as much time listening as talking. Remember that conversations are a two-way street. If we are nervous, we often go to one end of the spectrum by either talking too little or talking too much. Aim for the middle ground and you'll be fine.

- Be OK with being ignored. Accept that not everyone is willing to live the life that you might be creating for yourself. Don't take it personally if you try to start a conversation with someone at a bus queue and they turn their back on you. They would behave that way with everyone – it's not about you.

- Aim to ask open questions rather than only closed questions. Closed questions usually have one-word answers such as "Yes" or "No" and don't give you much room to develop a real conversation. They are only useful at the very beginning of a conversation, but they plant seeds for open questions to come. "It's warm today, isn't it?" is a closed question. They'll just say yes and leave you hanging. But if you follow it up with an open question, such as, "Any plans to enjoy it? Or are you going to be stuck inside too?", this will open things up for you to have a chat.

- Go out of your way to talk to someone in the supermarket. It's too easy to simply load your

EXERCISE

trolley, pay and walk away without saying a word
to anyone. Use the manned checkout rather than
self-service and speak to the staff there. Ask them if
they get a staff discount and whether it's worth you
applying for a job so as to get discounted bananas.

- Compliment someone. If someone's wearing a
blouse, carrying a bag, dyed their hair, or pierced
their entire face and it suits them, tell them so.
Ask them where they bought it or had it done and
open things up into a conversation.

- Look out for people walking their dog as an excuse
to say hello. Not only will it give you a chance to
chat but you might also get to pet a dog. Or better
still, get a dog yourself and go and take it for a walk.
I guarantee you'll have more "Good mornings"
thrown your way than you ever have had before.

- If you always sit with the same group of people in
the work canteen, deliberately sit with someone
else. Ask them how long they've worked there
and become more interested in them than you
usually would be. As the old phrase goes, "You can
make more friends in two months by becoming
interested in other people than you can in two
years trying to get other people interested in you."

Altruism

In a previous chapter, I've already spoken about the benefits of spending money on other people rather than spending it on yourself, but what if money's a bit tight? What can you do instead to have a significant impact upon your happiness? Do random acts of kindness have any genuine effect? Or do we just become a pushover that people take advantage of? Well, let's find out, shall we?

Studies[70] have long shown that there is a strong correlation between the happiness, health and even the longevity of people who are emotionally and behaviourally compassionate to others. Doing good makes you feel good, and it's often reported that the reason for this boost in happiness is because you feel you've influenced someone else's happiness for the better. But what if you don't?

Last year, I was in a supermarket checkout queue and was next in line to be served. The old lady in front of me had just had her little trolley of purchases scanned and she reached into her handbag to pay for her shopping when she suddenly gasped. She'd picked up the wrong purse; this one contained only a small amount of cash and no debit card. Would there be enough to pay for everything? Nope. She was £7 short and so had to make the uncomfortable decision of which items to leave behind, saying that she'd have to come back later for them. So, out go the sticky buns, the packet of bacon and the tin of tomatoes. She puts aside the Haribo, men's socks and Hobgoblin beer. What she decided to leave behind gave me a fascinating insight into her priorities, but that's another story. So, she wanders off to a windowsill shelf to pack up her things into a zip-up tartan shopping trolley. While she does that, I buy my handful of things and tell the cashier to scan her rejects too, which he does with a smile and I take them over to her. "For the sake of a few quid," I said to her, "I thought I'd save you having to come back later on."

She stared at me for a few seconds just working out whether to be suspicious of me or not and said, "But, how do I pay you back?" I told her that she didn't need to, that I'm just happy to help her out. I must have spent two minutes convincing her that there wasn't anything I was expecting in exchange. Eventually, she agreed that she'd done good by plenty of people throughout her life and deserved something back in return, so I was able to leave her alone to finish packing. But it made me question the idea of performing random acts of kindness.

Being kind to someone is always a great thing to do, obviously, but I think that the randomness of it can sometimes cause more negativity than we'd like. There's a big difference between letting a driver who's in the wrong lane cut in front of you and knocking on a stranger's door asking if they'd like you to clean their windows. The driver in the wrong lane is likely to think, "Thanks for that mate," whereas the stranger with the dirty windows is more likely to tell you to "bugger off and clean your own sodding windows". In a 21st-century society that often values self-preservation, someone being randomly kind to you looks suspicious. I wish it wasn't true and I know that if everyone in the country was reading this book and was prepared to help change the world, then things would be different. I'm afraid that's not the way it is, but you can still change some part of the world. Your world.

QUICK TIP

You may well have a few neighbours that struggle with mobility and would love you to take their dog for a walk every now and again. Connect with your neighbours through Nextdoor.com and find out who needs some help.

Or just simply pick up the phone and call someone you've not spoken to for a while, because that's a habit that it would be nice to get back into. It's a part of life that's being replaced with pixels on an electronic device, and that's not a proper conversation.

If you're going to incorporate altruism into your life, there's something important to bear in mind. Don't do it too often! Self-help books regularly suggest that daily random acts of kindness will make you a happier person. Research shows that it actually doesn't and that the whole daily kindness theory is a bit of a myth.[71] As with many things in life, if you do it too often, it becomes habitual and you don't even notice that you're doing it. Sure, there are behaviours that if they become part of your personality the world would be a better place. Hold a door open for someone, listen when someone is talking to you, stick your penny change in the charity tin, that sort of thing. You'll feel a little better about yourself, especially as you may well be inspiring others. But it's only when you reflect on it that it's likely to make you feel proud, and reflecting on your life and practising gratitude should make you feel pretty good anyway.

The reason why kindness boosts happiness is because it makes us feel worthwhile and appreciated within a community, satisfying our instinctive need to feel part of the tribe. It's important to recognise this because acting kind but feeling resentful won't boost your happiness, whereas doing anything that puts value on yourself will.

Leaving a sticky note on a bus window that says "Have a nice day!" is going to make someone smile and you will be contributing to their wellbeing. Knowing that you're having even this small a contribution to the upkeep of the world's mental health will also have an influence upon your own, but if you did this or something similar every day then the novelty will wear off.

There are some things in life that, from an evolutionary perspective, are great for the human race. Consuming high calories, having sex, keeping away from the edge of cliffs – these are activities that keep the species alive and so, over millions of years, natural selection favours the types of creatures that enjoy doing these sorts of things. One by one, each of the activities that are good for the continuation of the human race also begin to push happy buttons in the brain, and natural selection filters out the species that don't have the associations. They starve to death in the harsher winters, they don't have as many babies because they're not that interested in sex and they fall off cliffs.

The problem is that our brain has a very clever mechanism to save energy: it learns to cut corners. Corners that hundreds of thousands of years ago, we couldn't cut.

We don't know a massive amount about the sex lives of our prehistoric ancestors, but we do know that there is a correlation between libido and ovulation. If a woman is producing an egg, she's more likely to feel in the mood. But if we take a trip back in time, then our lean, low-in-body-fat, hunter-gathering women wouldn't become fertile until their late teens and would probably breastfeed for up to four years, preventing ovulation.

It's been suggested that despite a modern woman having 400 menstrual cycles in her lifetime, our ancient grannies probably didn't even have a dozen of them. So there's a possibility that we're having a heck of a lot more sex nowadays than we evolved to be expecting, and if something makes you feel good then your brain will make you desire it all the more. The thing is, our 'clever' brain realises that something has become routine and so doesn't produce the 'Ooh, that was good, do it again' signals. Basically anything that makes you feel good can become a habit and then it stops being fun.

It's the same for consuming calories and it's the same for feeling connected, valued, appreciated and safe. That's habituation and it is why if you take part in the idea of daily random acts of kindness, then you're not going to gain as much benefit as if you did all of them on a Monday instead. So, remember to be kind, but don't repeat the same acts of kindness all the time, because they will lose their influence on your happiness.

Assertiveness

Could you do me a favour?

I wonder if you could just drop everything you're doing for a bit and help me with something. Something that I think is important but not so important that I'll just get on with it myself – I'd much rather pass it on to you so that it's no longer my problem and also I've got someone to blame if it doesn't get done. Is that OK? Yes? Thank you.

Has that ever happened to you? Joining groups and being

a useful part of society can come at a cost if we forget about our own needs and damage our self-esteem.

I remember being a teenager and had not long started volunteering at my local hospital, when I had a phone call from one of the guys in charge, who asked me if I was able to do something one evening as he couldn't find anyone to do it. I said I couldn't, because I had family commitments, so he said, "Well, could you find someone who can then please." He passed the buck on to me and gave me a couple of names of people that he hadn't had a chance to ring. These were people I didn't even know and didn't have their phone number. When I told him this, he gave me some rough ideas of where they lived so that I could find them in the phone book and then he hung up.

At no point did I tell him that he was taking advantage of my altruistic attitude and that he should do it himself, as I now see that I should have done, or at least I should have told him to "bugger off". This sort of thing happened again and again for years and I can't quite remember how I snapped out of it, practising what I preach I think, as I was still a bit that way even after I qualified as a therapist. I remember, in my early years in the job, seeing clients that I really didn't have the time to see, that I should have referred on to someone with more time. But, as I mentioned in the self-esteem chapter, we feel a pull to be helpful and compliant.

Looking at some research done at the Max Planck Institute,[72] it seems that this can often go back a long way. Their research with toddlers showed that we are born wanting to help others and that we have to learn to be selfish. In one experiment when the researcher drops a clothes peg and can't reach it, the child will automatically jump up to help. But, if it's obvious that the researcher drops the peg on purpose, but still can't reach it, a huge majority of the time the toddler won't help. So yes, it is in our instincts to be altruistic, to look after each other, but not if they aren't prepared to look after themselves. Even an 18-month-old will see what's going on and not help. We need to do the same as adults, and learn to say no.

Whether it's to door-to-door sales people or sales calls on the phone, there are plenty of opportunities to practise. But remember, there's a difference between being assertive and being aggressive. When learning to be more assertive, people can sometimes forget that, and so it feels unrealistic to become that sort of character. But you don't need to be. Assertiveness is right in the middle between being passive and being aggressive. It enables you to be able to put your point across in such a way that it shouldn't anger the other person. That way, if they do become angry then you know that it's more of a reflection on them than on you.

LOOSE CHANGE IDEAS

In my dining room, I have a huge 4.5-litre brandy bottle that has long been drained of its drink and instead gets filled up with loose change. When full, it can hold quite a few hundred pounds in small change, and every now and again my son and I will tip some out and count out £50 before then deciding what to do with it.

EXERCISE

- If you don't have a stupidly huge brandy bottle in your house, you can even use a washed-out tin of soup. When filled with £1 coins, they can hold £200 quite easily.

- Put a £1 coin in it every Friday night. You could tip it out each Christmas and you've got £52 to play with.

- If you prefer the idea of getting rid of your small change, that old tin of soup when full of copper coins would easily raise a fiver.

- If you have children (hey, even if you don't) why not decorate a pipe of Pringles with some paint. Cut a hole into the lid and you have an ideal piggy bank that could easily hold £100 in small change.

- Many supermarkets have a self-service machine that counts out your change and gives you a receipt to cash in at the customer services desk. It comes at a cost though, usually 10%. Granted, there is an option to donate to some well-known charities instead, and for this they reduce their fees to only 7%. If this doesn't fit too well with you either, then nip into your bank or building society and pick up some plastic coin bags. Tip your change out onto the floor and count however much you want, bag it up and take it into your bank. The only difficult part is then deciding what to do with it.

WAYS OF MAKING A DIFFERENCE

- Kiva, the international non-profit organisation, is a great way of seeing your money put to use, and in the end it very often costs you nothing as you can usually get the money back again after it's been invested. If you've never heard of Kiva I'll give you a quick rundown. Someone, somewhere, is trying to start up a business, or needs a bit of cash to improve an existing business, for example starting up a market stall in Paraguay or building an extension to their school in Kenya. You contribute to a loan through Kiva and, as their business earns money, they pay it back to Kiva. Because they are funded through extra donations, sponsors and grants, Kiva are able to offer 0% interest on their loans. Once fully paid, Kiva then give it back to you, for you to either keep or reinvest with someone else. It's a great idea and will definitely make you feel as if you're contributing to making the world a better place. You can find more information at www.kiva.org.

- JustGiving.com have been around since 2001 and is a wonderful way of seeing just who is raising money and what they're doing to promote their favourite cause. You can donate money to a variety of different people. Recently I came across a Scout group taking part in a sponsored sleep out who were raising money to help homeless people get

EXERCISE

support with their mental health or housing needs. You could donate money to help a family cope with a breadwinner's sudden illness that leaves them struggling. Or donate to two drama students dressed in a pantomime horse costume running the London Marathon for Dogs for the Disabled. It genuinely is that varied, so there's plenty that might capture your interest.

- One way of finding out where the most efficient places to send money to is to use GiveWell. GiveWell is a non-profit organisation that investigates and evaluates charities. In doing so they are able to determine where money can be sent to in order to have the biggest influence on human lives per pound spent. If they can find a way that your £50 can have a dramatic effect on multiple lives, they'll show where it could go. For example, a charity that uses your money to buy insecticide-treated nets, to protect children in developing countries from malaria, has the potential to save dozens of lives. GiveWell will analyse the effectiveness of the charity, ensuring that the money is being distributed in all the right places for maximum effect. You can read about GiveWell at www. givewell.org and see their evidence-backed and thoroughly vetted list of organisations which are probably underfunded.

In recent years there have been many different charities advertising on TV and pulling at our heartstrings. But it's difficult to know exactly where would be an efficient organisation to send money to. For all I know, a charity raising money for a worthwhile cause may have staff that are paid twice the usual rate and only 1% of my donation ends up where it's actually needed. So it's worth doing a little bit of research.

Seeing what would happen to your donation in more detail will definitely have a greater impact on your wellbeing than simply dumping some pennies into the first charity collection tin you find.

Journal Suggestions

1. Who are the people in your life who will support you, and who can you genuinely trust?

2. Examine your values in life. What are the words you'd like to live by?

3. What's the one topic you need to learn more about to help you live a happier life?

4. Make a list of things you'd like to say no to.

5. Make a list of things you'd like to say yes to.

Chapter Eight:

Happy Ever After

In Conclusion

So, what is happiness?

You've invested all this time in this book so it's only fair that we try and sum it up somehow.

The point of this book might be to get you to change some of your beliefs and maybe that process has already started. But changing beliefs is more than just reading a book. You're going to need to challenge a lot of your thoughts over the next few weeks.

We've looked at the common ways that we think we can find happiness, and shown how wrong we are. But you may still think that having more money is the only thing that would make you happier. You need to challenge that.

If you're single and unhappy, then you might still think that the only way to be happy is to find the love of your life. You need to challenge that.

Perhaps you still think that if enough people say that they like you, you're going to be happy. You need to challenge that.

Maybe you're under-confident and think that the only way to be happy is to be the life and soul of the party. You need to challenge that.

In order to be truly happy, I believe that we need to stop putting so much faith in the thrills that give us only a temporary boost.

Having more money will only give us a temporary boost of happiness.

Falling in love is only a temporary boost.

Take opportunities in life that can thrill you by all means, but don't make thrill-seeking your goal.

How many happy drug addicts have you ever heard about? I doubt that you would actively seek the life of a drug addict. The negative consequences that go with it are awful. But, oh, the thrill! Those times of great pleasure! Someone addicted to heroin will sacrifice anything to get it. Despite the fact that they know full well it will only be a temporary high, they will do anything they can to get it.

Is that happiness? If it is, then drug addicts must be the happiest people on the planet.

Unfortunately, a lot of you will be living lives that aren't that different to this – it's just that the external thrill that you might seek is more acceptable to you than heroin is. But it's still external – it still requires something that could be taken away at some point.

If chilling out after work with a bottle of wine and watching the TV is your thrill, then you'll spend too much time wishing for it when you're experiencing something else.

When you're under pressure at work, all you'll want is the day to end so you can enjoy that bottle of wine.

Is that happiness? If so, then alcoholism must be the secret to being happy, and we know that it isn't. In fact, a happy alcoholic is one that doesn't drink alcohol any more.

Even love can be addictive. Meeting someone new is a thrill, it's exciting. But the effect wears off and either our flaws begin to show through or theirs do. If the negatives outweigh the positives in a relationship then we fall out of love and it comes to an end. But even if the positives outweigh the negatives, being addicted to the thrill will prevent us from being happy in the relationship, even though it's perfect.

Being addicted to any thrill at all will prevent us from being truly happy and may even make things worse. It's one thing to set our happiness on an upgraded phone once per year, but we can't upgrade our whole life. Most people can't realistically afford to upgrade their car every year. And almost nobody can afford to keep buying a bigger, better house every year.

As with a drug addict, the burdens that come with the addiction to thrill make for a very unhappy life.

The problem with having a human brain, though, is that we rarely think to ourselves, "You know, I need to find a better way of being happy." In fact, we don't tend to think anything at all. We just leave it to our habits and instincts to go after the next thrilling thing and then the next and then the next, and each time it doesn't make us any happier. If we do become aware of it, then we often think that we must be broken in some way because other people seem to be living this way and they're happy. But are they? You so often see in magazines that those people who seem to have everything are going into drug rehab. Yet they seem to have everything that we think we're searching for in order to be happy. They might have beauty, fame and fortune, but why do they then end up in drug rehab? Why do so many take their own lives? It's simply because that path of seeking happiness through things that are external never works.

Wishing and waiting for the next stimulus to poke our happy buttons won't make a permanent difference.

Thinking that it has to be home time for us to be happy means that we live for our evenings and nothing else. When that doesn't work, it leads us on to thinking that Friday is happy time and we live for our weekends. Every Monday then becomes our own personal hell and we soon become desperate for a holiday to get away from it all, counting down the weeks until the summer comes along when we can spend two weeks not thinking about work.

This leads us on to thinking we have to be retired to finally be contented, and we start wishing our life away, desperate to be in a position where we don't have to get out of bed if we don't want to.

Is this really being happy, because if it isn't then what is?

Well, I'll tell you, but you won't like it. After coming to the end of this book, what I say will hopefully make sense to you at some level. But you'll probably ignore me.

It is highly likely that you'll just go back to thrill-seeking again because most people do. Some of you won't and that's why I've written this book, for those of you that are willing to challenge yourselves and work at creating a life rather than just an existence.

It might be difficult to change, but if it was easy, everyone would be doing it. Society might try to convince you that it's not a good idea, even friends and family may try to convince you that I'm wrong because everyone's been persuaded to get onto the thrill-seeking treadmill to try and find pleasure in life. There's no money to be made in not seeking out the next shiny object and, unfortunately, money makes the world go round. Businesses are desperate for your money to satisfy their shareholders. In a world of 'On Demand' TV shows and the skipping of adverts, businesses are going to try even harder to convince you that you aren't happy without their new product.

So here's the answer, and remember, you're probably going to disagree at first, but if you go back to the start of this book and soak up all that I've taught you about how we work as humans, you'll see that it makes sense. But the answer to how to be happy is simply to recognise that, by default, you already are happy, even though there are things that happen that can make you forget that from time to time. When you realise that your happiness doesn't come from seeking out the next thrill but enjoying the thrills you already have, you will see that you are happy. Recognise that if you were to be reset to factory settings and start again you would be happy. You were born happy. There might have been things that happened to you that made you unhappy, but you quickly returned to being happy again very soon after. In your mother's womb, you were happy. You came out, one way or another, and felt cold and surprised and it made you unhappy, but you got used to it, became happy again and fell asleep.

Over the next few hours, days, weeks, months and years, happiness remained your default mode but occasionally something happened in your environment or in your mind that moved you from being happy to some other emotion. Occasionally you were anxious, angry or guilty, but you returned to being happy soon after. Sometimes you felt disappointed, pressured or frustrated. But later you forgot and became happy again. Over time, some of those other emotions may have become habitual and so it took less effort to create them, but there would have been times when you forgot to feel them and you were contented and happy.

When you can get out of your own way, you will find you are happy. People who meditate often say that while they're calm and settled they feel good. They quieten down that thrill-seeking part of them and feel happy. But the moment they stop meditating, all that thrill-seeking starts again and they return to their bad habits and bad feelings.

I'm not saying don't meditate, quite the opposite actually, please do. But in order for that happy state of mind to become the default again, you need to let go of the desire for the things that don't make you happy. Let go of the need to worry about what could go wrong. Let go of the need for that next shiny thing. Let go of needing to be liked by everyone.

Live a less intense life. A life without a huge focus on goals. A life almost without any desires at all. Sure, buy a new car every few years if you want to, but don't desire it. Buy it and enjoy it, appreciate it. But recognise that you'd have been happy anyway.

Recognise that things do go wrong in our lives, and it's fine to have an awareness of possible setbacks. But have faith in yourself that no matter how serious a problem you may encounter in your future, you'll be OK.

It may well still be important for you to achieve things

– please do. Go for that job promotion, ask that person to marry you, save up for that bigger house. Maybe do all the same things that you would have done if you'd never even found this book. But do them with less intensity, less addiction. Set things up so that your successes seem to simply happen by themselves with what seems like no effort at all, and allow life to just happen.

Forget about your setbacks and move on. Let go of any focus on your mistakes. Learn from them and move on.

Live almost like a child. Live in the present moment and focus more often on what's going on right now. Notice the simple things that ordinarily you'd filter out as unimportant. Notice the sounds of nature, notice how the wind affects the branches of the trees. Notice the people around you and the good in them. Notice something as simple as the way your breathing affects your body, the sensations in your nose, the movement of your chest.

Live the same life you would have done before finding this book if you like, but add quality to your life not quantity. If you're ready to evolve, if you're exhausted with the way you've been living before now and you're ready to move forward, then make these changes. It might be hard, it might take a lot of effort and it might take you a while to get there. But I promise you, it will be worth it.

Acknowledgements

First and foremost, I would like to thank Kelly Ellis from Blink Publishing for having confidence in my concepts and encouraging me to make them into a book. I am also incredibly grateful to Editors Oliver Holden-Rea and Nathan Joyce for their help in turning my haphazard jumble of ideas into a more coherent collection of sentences.

I am hugely grateful to all the scientists, researchers and psychologists who have dedicated so much time and effort to happiness research. This book would not have been possible without the likes of Daniel Kahneman, Sonja Lyubomirsky, Steven Pinker, Daniel Gilbert and Elizabeth Dunn who have inspired so many of us to check statistics and better understand the direction of causality so as not to give bad advice.

I'd also like to personally thank all of the therapy clients that I have worked with over the last 15 years, some truly wonderful people that have taught me more about mental health than books ever could.

Most of all I'd like to thank my wife and soul mate Dawn and my son Billy who have been, and will continue to always be, my best friends forever.

End Notes

1. Lykken, D. and Tellegen, A. (1996). Happiness is a stochastic phenomenon. *Psychological Science*, 7(3), pp.186-189.

2. Argyle, M. (1999). Causes and correlates of happiness. In D. Kahneman, E. Diener, & N. Schwarz (Eds.). *Well-being: The foundations of hedonic psychology*. New York: Russell Sage Foundation, pp.353-373.

3. Wegner, D. (1989). *White bears and other unwanted thoughts: Suppression, obsession, and the psychology of mental control*. New York: Viking.

4. Pham, L. and Taylor, S. (1999). From thought to action: Effects of process- versus outcome-based mental simulations on performance. *Personality and Social Psychology Bulletin*, 25(2), pp.250-260.

5. Pennebaker, J. and Chung, C. (in press). (2007). Expressive writing and its link to mental and Physical health. In H.S. Friedman (Eds), *Oxford Handbook of Health Psychology*. New York, NY: Oxford University Press.

6. Baumeister, R. and Tierney, J. (2012). *Willpower: Rediscovering the Greatest Human Strength*. New York: Penguin Books.

7. Clifton, J. (2017). The Happiest and Unhappiest Countries in the World. Retrieved from http://www.gallup.com/opinion/gallup/206468/happiest-unhappiest-countries-world.aspx.

8. Mauss, I., Tamir, M., Anderson, C., Savino, N. (2011). Can seeking happiness make people unhappy? Paradoxical effects of valuing happiness. *Emotion*, 11(4), pp.807-815.

9. Lane, R. and Schwartz, G. (1987). Levels of emotional awareness: A cognitive-developmental theory and its application to psychopathology. *American Journal of Psychiatry*, 144(2), pp.133-143.

    Lindquist, K. and Barrett, L. (2008). Emotional complexity. In Lewis, M., Haviland-Jones, J. and Barrett, L. (Eds.). *The Handbook of Emotions*, 3rd edition. New York, NY: Guilford, pp.513–530.

10. Piff, P., Stancato, D., Côté, S., Mendoza-Denton, R. and Keltner, D. (2012). Higher social class predicts increased unethical behavior. *Proceedings of the National Academy of Sciences*, 109(11), pp.4086-4091.

11. Vohs, K., Mead, N. and Goode, M. (2006). The Psychological Consequences of Money. American Association for the Advancement of Science. *Science* 17(314), Issue 5802, pp.1154-1156.

12. Kahneman, D. and Deaton A. (2010). High Income Improves Evaluation of Life but Not Emotional Well-Being. *Proceedings of the National Academy of Sciences*, 107(38), pp.16489-93.

13. Brickman, P., Coates, D. and Janoff-Bulman, R. (1978). Lottery winners and accident victims: Is happiness relative? *Journal of Personality and Social Psychology*, 36(8), pp.917-927.

14. Stutzer, A. and Frey, B. (2004). Stress That Doesn't Pay: The Commuting Paradox. IEW - Working Papers 151, Institute for Empirical Research in Economics – University of Zurich.

15. Brochet, F. and Morrot, G. (1999). Influence of the context on the perception of wine – Cognitive and methodological implications. *Journal International des Sciences de la Vigne et du Vin*, 33, pp.187-192.

16. Brochet, F. and Morrot, G. (2001). The Color of Odors. *Brain and Language*, 79(2), pp.309-320.

17. Fritz, C., Curtin, J., Poitevineau, J. and Tao, F-C. (2017). Social Sciences – Psychological and Cognitive Sciences – Physical Sciences – Engineering: Listener evaluations of new and Old Italian violins. *PNAS 2017*, 114(21), pp.5395-5400, doi:10.1073/pnas.1619443114.

18. Dunn, E., Aknin, L. and Norton, M. (2008). Spending money on others promotes happiness. Science, 319(5870), pp.1687–1688.

19. Whillans, A., Dunn, E., Smeets, P., Bekkers, R. and Norton, M. (2017). Buying Time Promotes Happiness. *Proceedings of the National Academy of Sciences*, 114(32), 201706541. doi:10.1073/pnas.1706541114.

20. Chaplin, L. and John, D. (2007). Growing up in a material world: Age differences in materialism in children and adolescents. *Journal of Consumer Research*, 34(4), pp.480–493.

21. Floyd, K., Mikkelson, A., Hesse, C. and Pauley, P. (2007). Affectionate writing reduces total cholesterol: Two randomized, controlled trials. *Human Communication Research*, 33(2), pp.119-142.

22. King, L. (2001). The health benefits of writing about life goals. *Personality and Social Psychology Bulletin*, 27(7), pp.798-807.

23. Larsen, J. and McKibban A. (2008). Is Happiness Having What You Want, Wanting What You Have, or Both? *Psychological Science*, 19(4), pp.371-77, doi:10.1111/j.1467-9280.2008.02095.x.

24. Killingsworth, M. and Gilbert, D. (2010). A Wandering Mind Is an Unhappy Mind. *Science*, 330(6006), pp.932-932, doi:10.1126/science.1192439.

25. Lazar, S. et al. (2005). Meditation experience is associated with increased cortical thickness. *NeuroReport* 16(17), pp.1893-1897.

26. Hölzel B., Carmody J., Vangel M., Congleton C., Yerramsetti S., Gard T. and Lazar S.W. (2011). Mindfulness practice leads to increases in regional brain gray matter density. *Psychiatry Research*, 191(1), pp.36-43.

27. Davidson, R., Kabat-Zinn, J., Schumacher, J., Rosenkranz, M., Muller, D., Santorelli, S., Urbanowski, F., Harrington, A., Bonus, K. and Sheridan, J. (2003). Alterations in brain and immune function produced by mindfulness meditation. *Psychosomatic Medicine*, 65(4), pp.564-570.

28. Kross, E., Berman, M., Mischel, W., Smith, E. and Wager, T. (2011). Social Rejection Shares Somatosensory Representations with Physical Pain. *Proceedings of the National Academy of Sciences* 108(15), pp.6270-6275, doi:10.1073/pnas.1102693108.

29. Leary, M., Kowalski, R., Smith, L. and Phillips, S. (2003). Teasing, Rejection, and Violence: Case Studies of the School Shootings. *Aggressive Behavior*, 29, pp.202-214, doi:10.1002/ ab.10061.

30. Darley, J. and Gross, P. (1983). A hypothesis-confirming bias in labeling effects. *Journal of Personality and Social Psychology*, 44(1), pp.20-33.

31. Snyder, M., Tanke, E. and Berscheid, E. (1977). Social Perception and Interpersonal Behavior: On the Self-Fulfilling Nature of Social Stereotypes. *Journal of Personality and Social Psychology*, 35, pp.656-666.

32. Rosenthal, R. and Jacobson, L. (1966). Teachers' expectancies: Determinants of pupils' IQ gains. *Psychological Reports*, 19, pp.115-118.

33. Pelham, B., Mirenberg, M. and Jones, J. (2002). Why Susie sells seashells by the seashore: Implicit egotism and major life decisions. *Journal of Personality and Social Psychology*, 82(4), pp.469-487.

34. Jones, J., Pelham, B., Carvallo, M. and Mirenberg M. (2004). How do I love thee? Let me count the Js: implicit egotism and interpersonal attraction. *Journal of Personality and Social Psychology*, 87(5), pp.665-683.

35. Wood, J., Perunovic, E. and Lee, J. (2009). Positive Self-Statements: Power for Some, Peril for Others. *Psychological Science*, 20(7), pp.860-866, DOI: 10.1111/j. 467-9280.2009.02370.x.

36. Eisenstadt, D. and Leippe, M. (1994). The self-comparison process and self-discrepant feedback: Consequences of learning

you are what you thought you were not. *Journal of Personality and Social Psychology*, 67(4), pp.611-626.

37. Hartnett, J. and Skowronski, J. (2010). Affective forecasts and the Valentine's Day shootings at NIU: People are resilient, but unaware of it. *Journal of Positive Psychology*, 5(4), pp.275-280, DOI:10.1080/17439760.2010.498615.

38. Sharp, E. and Ganong, L. (2011). I'm a Loser, I'm Not Married, Let's Just All Look at Me: Ever-Single Women's Perceptions of Their Social Environment. *Journal of Family Issues*, 32(7), pp.956-980, doi:10.1177/0192513X10392537.

39. Luhmann, M., Hofmann, W., Eid, M. and Lucas, R. (2012). Subjective Well-Being and Adaptation to Life Events: A Meta-Analysis. *Journal of Personality and Social Psychology*, 102(3), pp.592-615, doi:10.1037/a0025948.

40. DePaulo, B. (2007) Singled Out. New York, NY: St. Martin's Press.

41. Clark, A., Diener, E., Georgellis, Y. and Lucas, R. (2008). Lags and leads in life satisfaction: A test of the baseline hypothesis. *Economic Journal*, 118, pp.222-243.

42. Festinger, L. and Carlsmith, J. (1959). Cognitive Consequences of Forced Compliance. *Journal of Abnormal Psychology*, 58(2), pp.203-10.

43. Kirby, P. (2015). Levels of Success: The Potential of UK Apprenticeships. The Sutton Trust.

44. Sakulku, J. (2011). The Imposter Phenomenon. *International Journal of Behavioral Science*, 6(1), pp.73-92.

End Notes

45. Kruger, J. and Dunning, D. (1999). Unskilled and Unaware of It: How Difficulties in Recognizing One's Own Incompetence Lead to Inflated Self-Assessments. *Journal of Personality and Social Psychology*, 77(6): pp.1121-1134.

46. Strack, F., Martin, L. and Stepper, S. (1988). Inhibiting and Facilitating Conditions of the Human Smile: A Nonobtrusive Test of the Facial Feedback Hypothesis. *Journal of Personality and Social Psychology*, 54(5), pp.768-777.

47. Schnall, S. and Laird, J. (2003). Keep smiling: Enduring effects of facial expressions and postures on emotional experience. *Cognition and Emotion*, 17, pp.787-797.

48. Wollmer, M., de Boer, C., Kalak, N., Beck, J., Götz, T., Schmidt, T., Hodzic, M., Bayer, U., Kollmann, T., Kollewe, K., Sönmez, D., Duntsch, K., Haug, M., Schedlowski M., Hatzinger, M., Dressler, D., Brand, S., Holsboer-Trachsler, E. and Kruger, T. (2012). Facing depression with botulinum toxin: A randomized controlled trial. *Journal of Psychiatric Research*, 46(5), pp.574-581.

49. Carney, D., Cuddy, A. and Yap. (2015). A. Review and Summary of Research on the Embodied Effects of Expansive (vs. Contractive) Nonverbal Displays. *Psychological Science*, 26(5), pp.657-663.

50. Cuddy, A., Wilmuth, C., Yap, A. and Carney, D. (2015). Preparatory power posing affects nonverbal presence and job interview performance. *Journal of Applied Psychology*, 100(4), pp.1286-1295.

51. Diener, E., Pressman, S., Hunter, J. and Delgadillo-Chase, D. (2017). If, Why, and When Subjective Well-Being Influences Health, and Future Needed Research. *Applied Psychology: Health and Well-Being*, 9(2), pp.133-167, doi:10.1111/aphw.12090.

52. Broadbent, E., Kahokehr, A., Booth, R., Thomas, J., Windsor, J., Buchanan, C. et al. (2012). A brief relaxation intervention reduces stress and improves surgical wound healing response: A randomised trial. *Brain, Behavior, and Immunity*, 26, pp.212-217. https://doi.org/10.1016/j.bbi.2011.06.014

53. Basso, J. and Suzuki, W. (2017). The Effects of Acute Exercise on Mood, Cognition, Neurophysiology, and Neurochemical Pathways: A Review. *Brain Plasticity* 2(2), pp.127-52, doi:10.3233/BPL-160040.

54. Angadi, S., Weltman, A., Watson-Winfield, D., Weltman, J., Frick, K., Patrie, J. and Gaesser, G. (2010). Effect of fractionized vs continuous, single-session exercise on blood pressure in obese and non-obese adults. *Journal of Human Hypertension*, 24, pp.300-302.

55. Bouchard, C., and Tremblay, A. (1997). Genetic influences on the response of body fat and fat distribution to positive and negative energy balances in human identical twins. *Journal of Nutrition*, 127(5), pp.943S-947S.

56. Ravussin, E. et al. (1986). Determinants of 24-hour energy expenditure in man. Methods and results using a respiratory chamber. *Journal of Clinical Investigation*, 78(6), pp.1568-1578.

57. Miller, M., King, L., Camerer, C. and Rangel, A. (2010). Pavlovian processes in consumer choice: The physical presence of a good increases willingness-to-pay. *American Economic Review*, 100(4), pp.1556-1571.

58. Levitsky, D. and Youn, T. (2004). The More Food Young Adults Are Served, the More They Overeat. *Journal of Nutrition*, 134(10), pp.2546-2549.

59. Wansink, B., Painter, J. and North, J. (2005). Bottomless Bowls: Why Visual Cues of Portion Size May Influence Intake. *Obesity Research*, 13(1), pp.93-100, doi:10.1038/oby.2005.12.

60. Laran, J. and Salerno, A. (2013). Life-History Strategy, Food Choice, and Caloric Consumption. *Psychological Science*, 24(2) pp.167-173, doi:10.1177/0956797612450033.

61. Geier, A., Rozin, P. and Doros, G. (2006). Unit Bias: A New Heuristic That Helps Explain the Effect of Portion Size on Food Intake. *Psychological Science*, 17(6), pp.521-525.

62. Andrade, A., Greene, G. and Melanson K. (2008). Eating slowly led to decreases in energy intake within meals in healthy women. *Journal of the American Dietetic Association*, 108(7), pp.1186-1191, 10.1016/j.jada.2008.04.026.

63. Karine S., Leproult, R., L'Hermite-Balériaux, M., Copinschi, G., Penev, P. and Van Cauter, E. (2004). Leptin Levels Are Dependent on Sleep Duration: Relationships with Sympathovagal Balance, Carbohydrate Regulation, Cortisol, and Thyrotropin. *Journal of Clinical Endocrinology & Metabolism* 89, pp.5762-5771.

64. Lieberman, M. (2016). *Social*. Broadway Books.

65. House, J., Landis, K. and Umberson, D. (1988). Social Relationships and Health. *Science*, 241(4865), pp.540-545, doi:10.1126/science.3399889.

66. McPherson, M., Smith-Lovin, L. and Brashears, M. (2006). Social Isolation in America: Changes in Core Discussion Networks over Two Decades. *American Sociological Review*, 71(3), pp.353-375, doi:10.1177/000312240607100301.

67. Shakya, H. and Christakis, N. (2017). Association of Facebook Use With Compromised Well-Being: A Longitudinal Study. *American Journal of Epidemiology*, 185(3), pp.203-211, doi:10.1093/aje/kww189.

68. Kross, E., Verduyn, P., Demiralp, E., Park, J., Lee, D., Lin, N., Shablack, H., Jonides, J. and Ybarra, O. (2013). Facebook Use Predicts Declines in Subjective Well-Being in Young Adults. PLOS ONE, 8(8), doi:10.1371/journal.pone.0069841.

69. Epley, N. and Schroeder, J. (2014). Mistakenly Seeking Solitude. *Journal of Experimental Psychology*, General 143(5), pp.1980-1999, doi:10.1037/a0037323.

70. Post, S. (2005). Altruism, Happiness, and Health: It's Good to Be Good. *International Journal of Behavioral Medicine*, 12(2), pp.66-77, doi:10.1207/s15327558ijbm1202_4.

71. Lyubomirsky, S., Sheldon, K. and Schkade, D. (2005). Pursuing happiness: The architecture of sustainable change. *Review of General Psychology*, 9, pp.111-131.

72. Warneken, F. and Tomasello, M. (2006). Altruistic Helping in Human Infants and Young Chimpanzees. Science, 311(5765), pp.1301-1303.